Art
And Math

Throughout the Year

by Jimmie Aydelott

Fearon Teacher Aids
Belmont, California

✦✦✦

Entire contents copyright © 1989 by Fearon Teacher Aids, 500 Harbor
Boulevard, Belmont, California 94002. However, the individual purchaser
may reproduce designated materials in this book for classroom and individual
use, but the purchase of this book does not entitle reproduction of any part
for an entire school, district, or system. Such use is strictly prohibited.

ISBN 0-8224-0104-5

Printed in the United States of America

1. 9 8 7 6 5 4 3 2

Contents

Introduction 5

"Nutty" September 6–13
    Acorn Count   (K)
    Can You Picture That?   (1–2) *add. + sub. facts*
    "Nutty" Book   (3)
    Think About It . . .   (4–6)

"Batty" October 14–19
    Five Little Bats   (K)
    Bat Mobile   (1–2) *fact families*
    Bat-O-Graph   (3)
    Think About It . . .   (4–6)

November Turkey Time 20–26
    Mr. Turkey   (K)
    More Turkey Please!   (1–2) *</>*
    Turkey Weigh-In   (3)
    Think About It . . .   (4–6)

Delightful "Decem-bear" 27–34
    Gifts Galore!   (K)
    Bear-y Good Gifts   (1–2) *counting money*
    Wish Book   (3)
    Think About It . . .   (4–6)

January "Snow" Biz 35–42
    Snowman Count   (K)
    Snowball Sculpture   (1–2) *measurement*
    Blizzard Bunch   (3)
    Think About It . . .   (4–6)

Heart-y February Fun! 43–49
    Hearts, Hearts, Hearts   (K)
    Happy Hearts   (1–2) *union of sets*
    "Heart-y" Party   (3)
    Think About It . . .   (4–6)

March/April Funny Bunnies 50–57
    Funny Bunny Families   (K)
    Egg Hunt   (1–2) *Number patterns*
    Funny Bunny Fractions   (3)
    Think About It . . .   (4–6)

May Blooming Brightly 58–64
    Petal Power   (K)
    Flower Fun   (1–2) *Pictographs*
    Spring Things   (3)
    Think About It . . .   (4–6)

Introduction

Art and Math Throughout the Year provides multilevel math lessons presented in an art project format. Many projects are designed for bulletin board displays. Ideas are given on how to use the bulletin boards as teaching tools for "teaching off the wall."

Each unit is centered around a monthly theme and begins with four math lessons. Each lesson indicates the grade it is best suited for (K–6) and the math concept presented in the lesson. Keep in mind that lessons can be easily adapted to cover a broader age range, and they need not be limited to the grade level suggested. Problem solving is a skill that requires constant reinforcement, and so lessons suggested for the upper elementary grades are all centered around seasonal word problems.

Each unit also contains a seasonal fill-in worksheet. Fill the worksheet with math problems that reinforce your current unit of study and duplicate it for each student.

To assist with bulletin board displays, most units have a border pattern. To make a colorful, seasonal border, cut 6" x 18" strips of construction paper. Cut as many strips as necessary to enclose your display area. Fold each strip into four equal sections. Trace the border pattern onto the folded strip and cut it out. Repeat until all strips have been cut. This is a good project for student helpers.

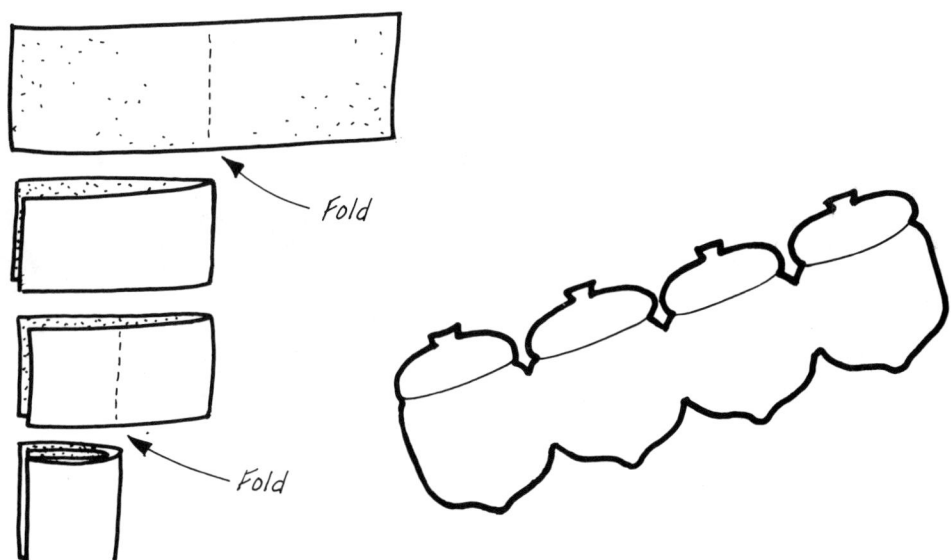

Each unit provides a bulletin board idea for displaying student work. Also, many units have a special art project students can make to display their own individual math papers.

Art and Math Throughout the Year can help you have colorful student-created room displays and further your students' excitement for learning math.

"Nutty" SEPTEMBER

Math Lessons

Acorn Count
Kindergarten
concept: *counting*
Write a number word or counting dots on the top of each acorn pattern (page 10) before duplicating and then give one sheet to each student. Let the students cut out the acorns and write the correct number on each one. Display the acorns on a "We're Nutty About Numbers" bulletin board along with the enlarged squirrel (page 9). Have the squirrel hold a number and then ask the students to tell which acorns on the board are the same number as the one the squirrel is holding. Or, have the students tell which acorns are one more or one less. Allow the children to take home their acorns to use as flashcards.

Can You Picture That?
First and Second Grade
concept: *addition and subtraction facts*
Write a number fact on each acorn (page 10) and represent it with pictures before duplicating. Let children either cross out for subtraction or circle for addition to show their understanding of the facts. Children can color and cut out the acorns.

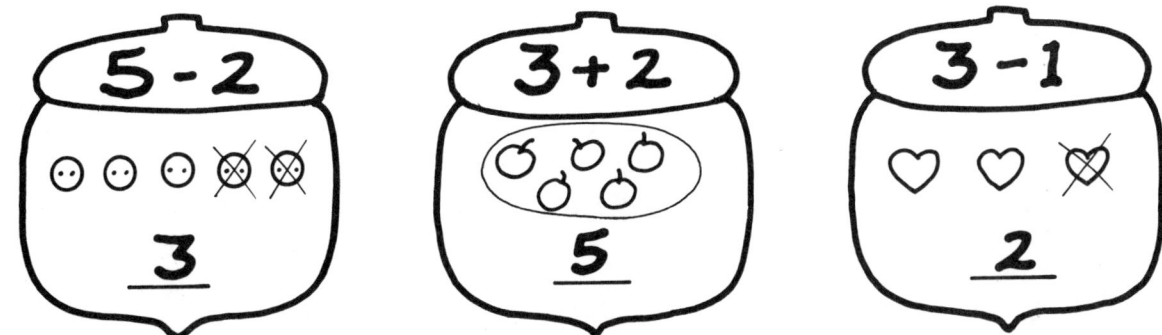

"Nutty" September

Math Lessons

"Nutty" Book
Third Grade
concept: *word problems*

Duplicate enough large acorn patterns (page 13) for each child to have several. Let students make up word problems or use some suggested below. Have children write one problem on each acorn and staple them together with a cover to create word problem booklets. The students can print the answers upside down or on the back of each acorn. Extra acorn pages can be added so that students can illustrate their word problems.

1. Sammy Squirrel worked at the Nut House 2 hours on Monday, 3 hours on Tuesday, 4 hours on Wednesday, 4 hours on Thursday, and 3 hours on Friday. How many hours did he work in all?
2. Susie Squirrel gathered 57 acorns. Scottie Squirrel gathered 32. How many more did Susie gather than Scottie?
3. Sadie Squirrel gathered 13 nuts and Stanley Squirrel gathered a dozen nuts. Who gathered more? How many more?
4. Sabrina gathered 98 nuts. She gave 12 to Shelly Squirrel. Then she gathered 10 more. How many does she have now?
5. If Sharon Squirrel paid $2.00 for one can of salted nuts, how much would two cans cost?
6. Sara Squirrel stored 428 nuts for winter. Rounded to the nearest 100, how many nuts did she store?

Think About It . . .
Fourth, Fifth, and Sixth Grade
concept: *word problems*

1. Shelby Squirrel gathered 20 nuts Monday, 50 Tuesday, 60 Wednesday, 70 Thursday 30 Friday. What was the average for the week?
2. Shirley Squirrel and Sybil Squirrel picked 24 bags of peanuts. Shirley picked twice as many as Sybil. How many bags did Sybil pick?
3. Sherman Squirrel works at the Nut House. He is paid $3.50 per hour. He works 40 hours a week. How much will he earn in 9 weeks?
4. Sally Squirrel is making pecan pies. She uses 200 pecans for one pie. How many will she use in a dozen pies?
5. Sidney Squirrel has 2 dozen more nuts than Sylvester Squirrel who has 1 dozen acorns, 2 dozen pecans, 2 dozen walnuts, and 1 dozen hazelnuts. How many nuts does Sidney have?

Math Lessons

6. Samantha Squirrel bought 5 pounds of acorns for $25.00. How much per pound did she pay?

7. Sigmund Squirrel has 478 acorns, 221 hazelnuts, 89 pecans, and 598 walnuts. How many nuts does Sigmund have in all?

8. The Scott Squirrel family started nut hunting at 6:00 A.M. Saturday and stopped at 6:00 P.M. They had a 15-minute rest break in the morning and another in the afternoon. Their lunch period was from 1:00 to 2:30. How many hours did they hunt nuts?

Word problems can be displayed for further practice. Enlarge the squirrel pattern below. Cut his tail from furry cloth. Write a problem on his acorn. Students can help make squirrels and add other details to make a "nutty" bulletin board.

Acorn Patterns

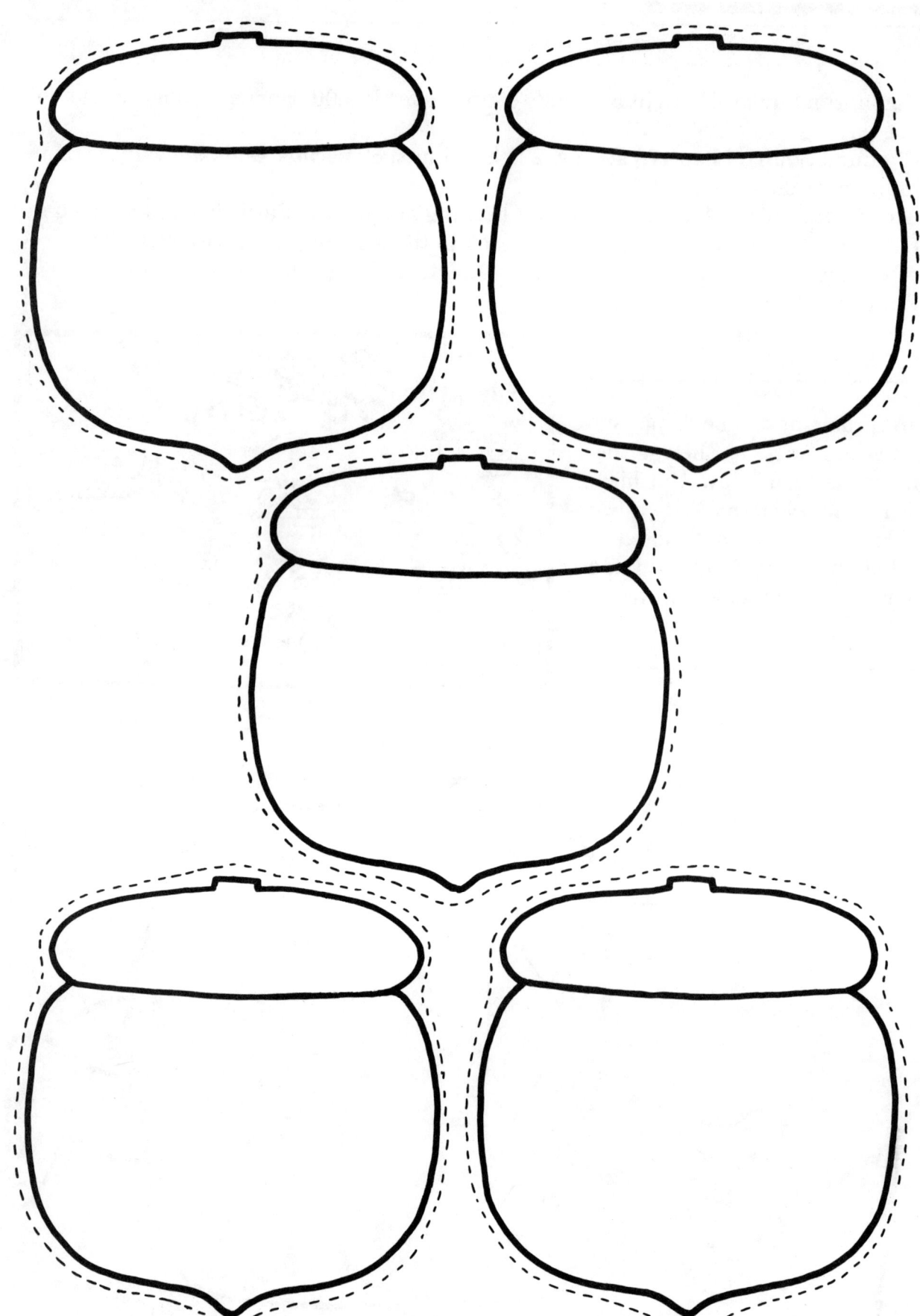

10 *"Nutty" September*

Name: _____

I'm Nutty About Math
✣ ✣ ✣
Solve the problems. Check your work.

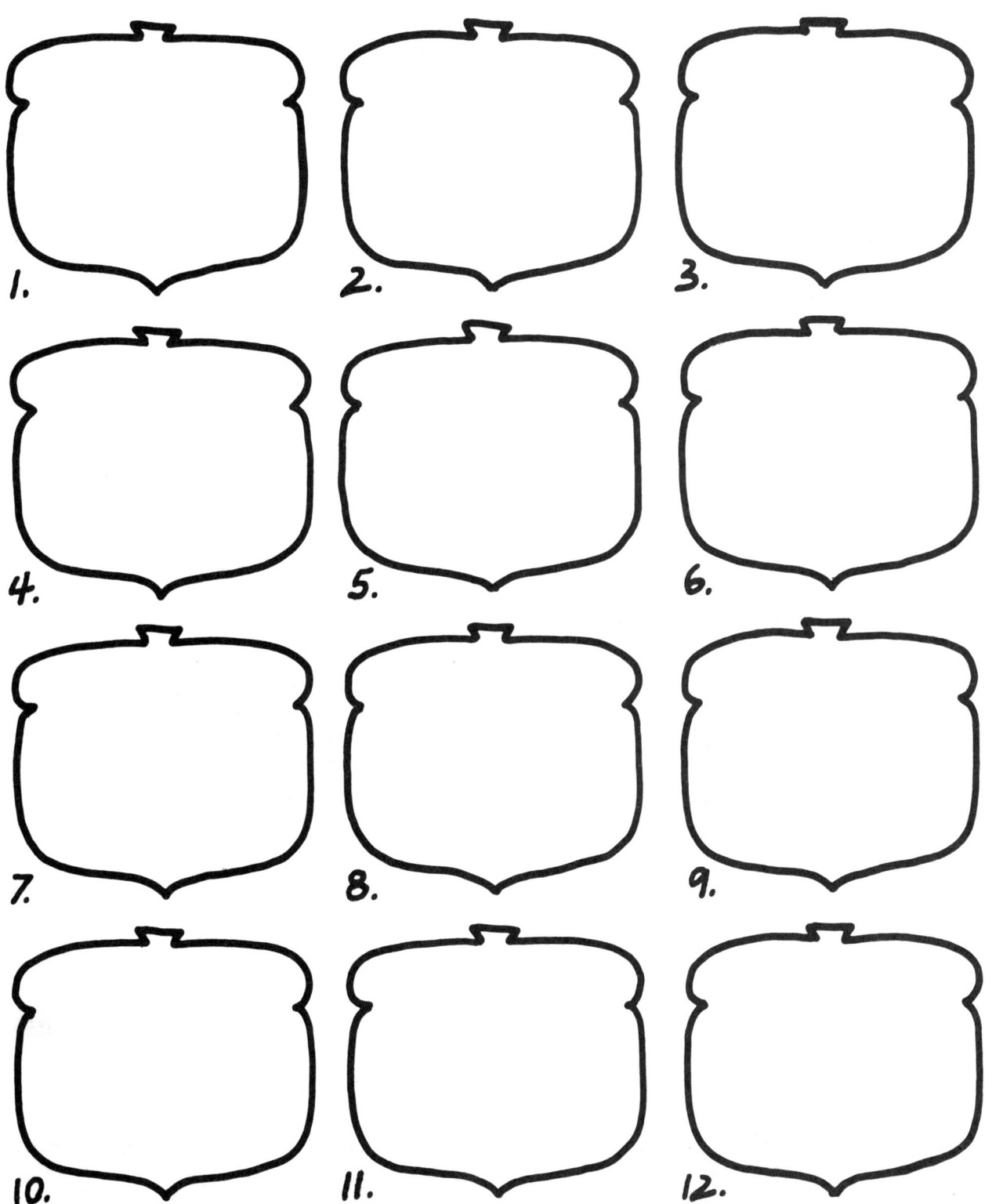

"Nutty" September

Peek-Over Squirrel

Directions: Color the two parts of the picture. Cut on the dotted lines. Glue the four corners of your math paper on a sheet of colored construction paper. Glue the squirrel's head on the left corner. Glue its feet at the bottom. Be sure the feet are under its body.

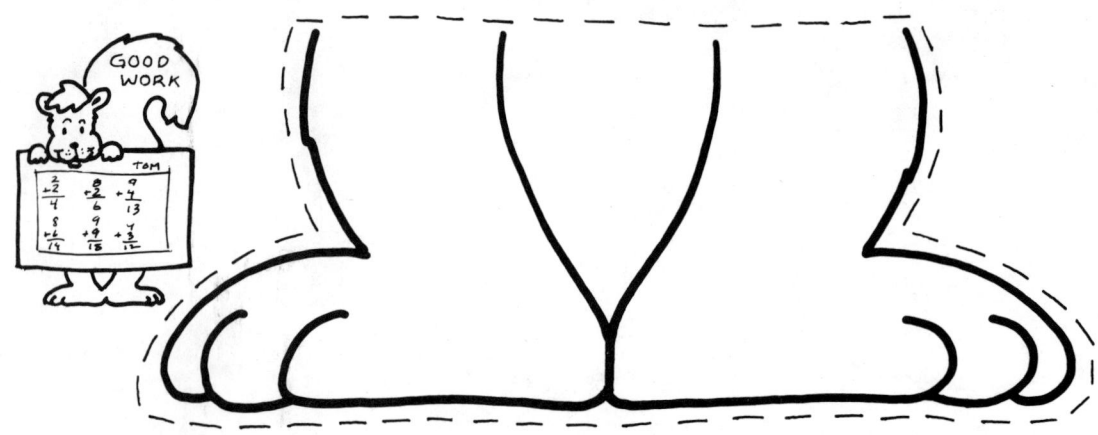

12 "Nutty" September

Border Pattern

place on fold

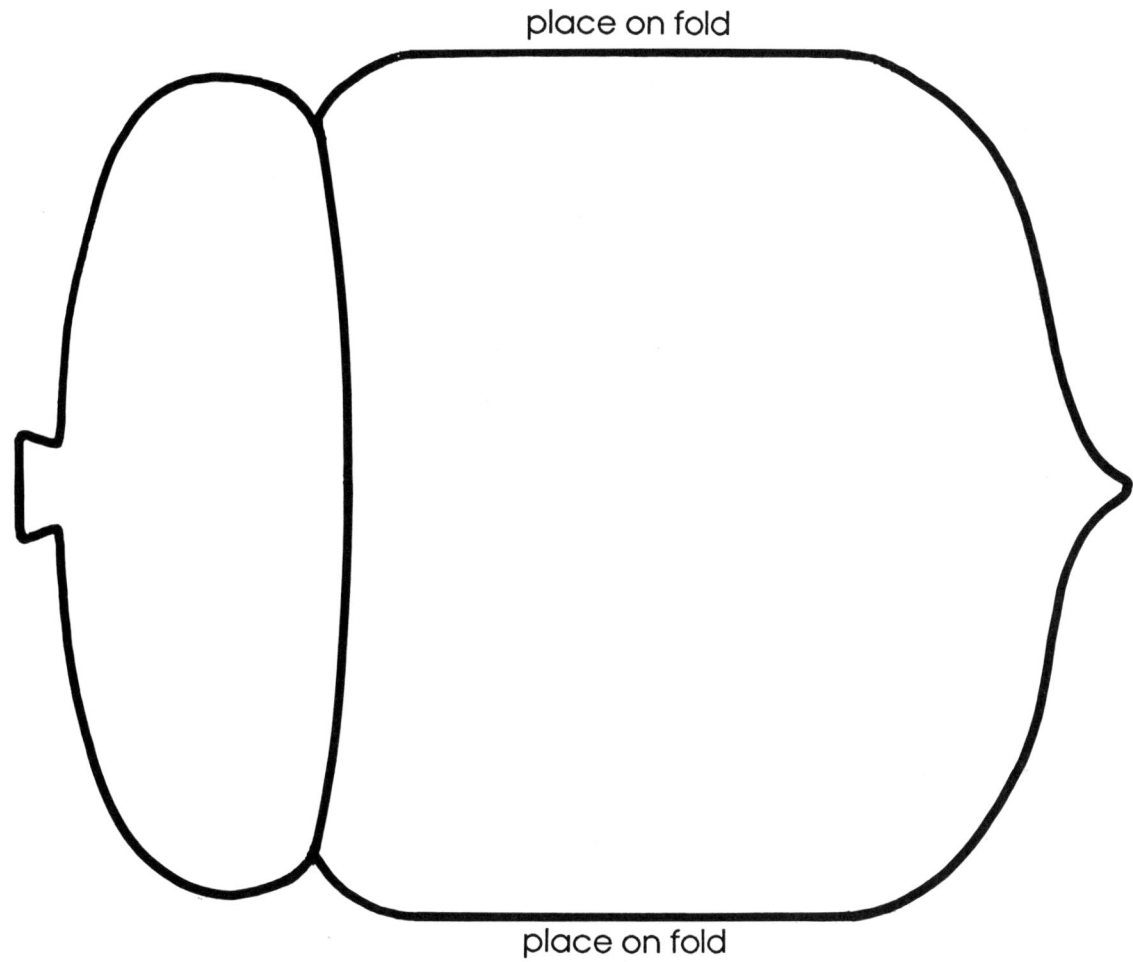

place on fold

Good Work Display

Enlarge the "peek-over" squirrel and have him peek over the whole bulletin board. Trim with the acorn border pattern and scatter a few fall leaves.

"Nutty" September

"Batty"
OCTOBER

Math Lessons

Five Little Bats
Kindergarten
concept: *adding "one more"*
Give each child six 6" yellow circles and a copy of "Five Little Bats" (page 17). Let each child cut the poem and bats apart on the dotted lines. Poem piece #1 should be glued on a yellow moon with one bat. Poem piece #2 should be glued on a moon with two bats and so on. Use the sixth moon to make a cover. Staple together to make a booklet.

Bat Mobile
First and Second Grade
concept: *"family" number facts*
Give each child a bat body and wing pattern (page 19). Using black construction paper, have each child trace and cut out three bodies and six wings. Two or three pieces of paper can be stacked together to cut out more than one pattern at a time. Let children glue the wings on the three bats and write a different number on each bat body using white chalk. The three numbers should be related numbers that can be used to make four number sentences.

    Example: 2, 3, 5
       3 + 2 = 5
       2 + 3 = 5
       5 - 2 = 3
       5 - 3 = 2

Have children write the four number sentences on a 5" yellow circle. Using thread, suspend the "moon" and three bats from a clothes hanger to complete the "Bat Mobile."

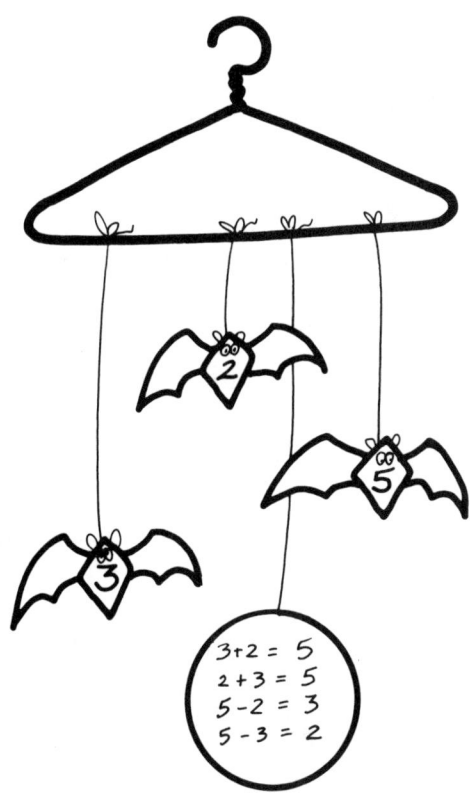

"Batty" October

Math Lessons

Bat-O-Graph
Third Grade
concept: *pictographs*

Using the pattern on page 19, let each student make one bat with large white eyes. (Use 1/2" white circles to glue on black bat.) Children can color the eyes on their bats brown, blue, red, green, or yellow. Display bats on a bulletin board and ask the following questions:

1. How many bats have blue eyes?
2. What is the difference in the number of bats with green eyes and the number with yellow eyes?
3. Which is greater, blue-eyed bats + brown-eyed bats or green-eyed bats + red-eyed bats?
4. How many bats does each picture represent?

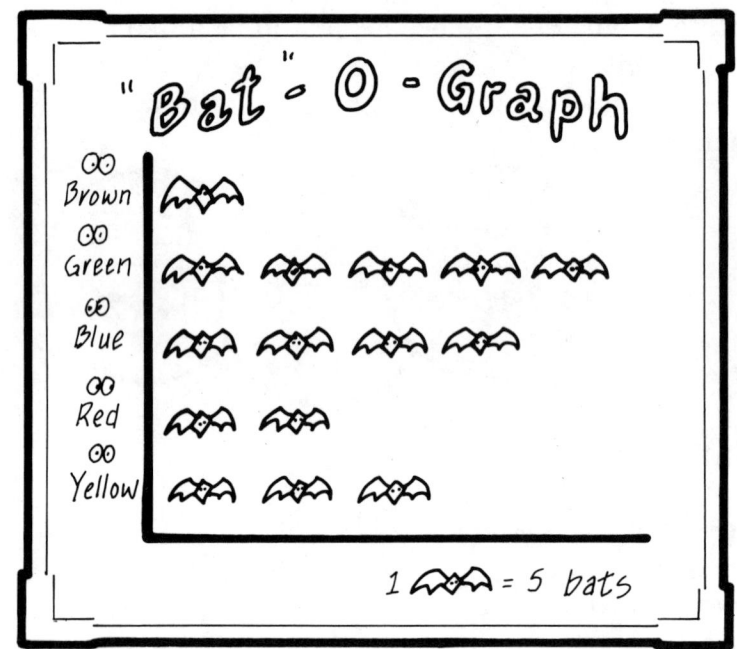

Think About It...
Fourth, Fifth, and Sixth Grade
concept: *word problems*

1. There were 20 bats in Cabot Cave. One-fourth flew away. How many were left?
2. Baby Billy Bat sleeps 20 hours a day. How many hours is he awake?
3. Betty Bat can fly 10 miles per hour. How long will it take her to fly 30 miles at that speed?
4. Bobby Bat left his cave at 8:00 P.M. He arrived at the haunted house at 11:58 P.M. How long did he fly?
5. Big Bertram Bat has a wing span of 21 inches. Buddy Bat's wing span is 2 1/2 feet. What is the difference?
6. Big Bertha Bat ate 9 out of 10 pieces of Batpizza Supreme. What fractional part did she eat? What part was left?
7. Barbara Bat worked at the haunted house cafeteria for 2 hours and 15 minutes. She arrived at 10:00 P.M. What time did she leave?

Five Little Bats

1 One little bat went out to fly.
Soon another darted by.

2 One little bat and another little bat
Gives us two—just like that!

3 Two little bats and one more—Just watch these three soar and soar.

4 Now three bats and another one,
Make four little bats just out for fun.

5 Four little bats and one more tonight.
Now five little bats—oh, what a fright!

Cut apart on dotted lines and glue on yellow moons.

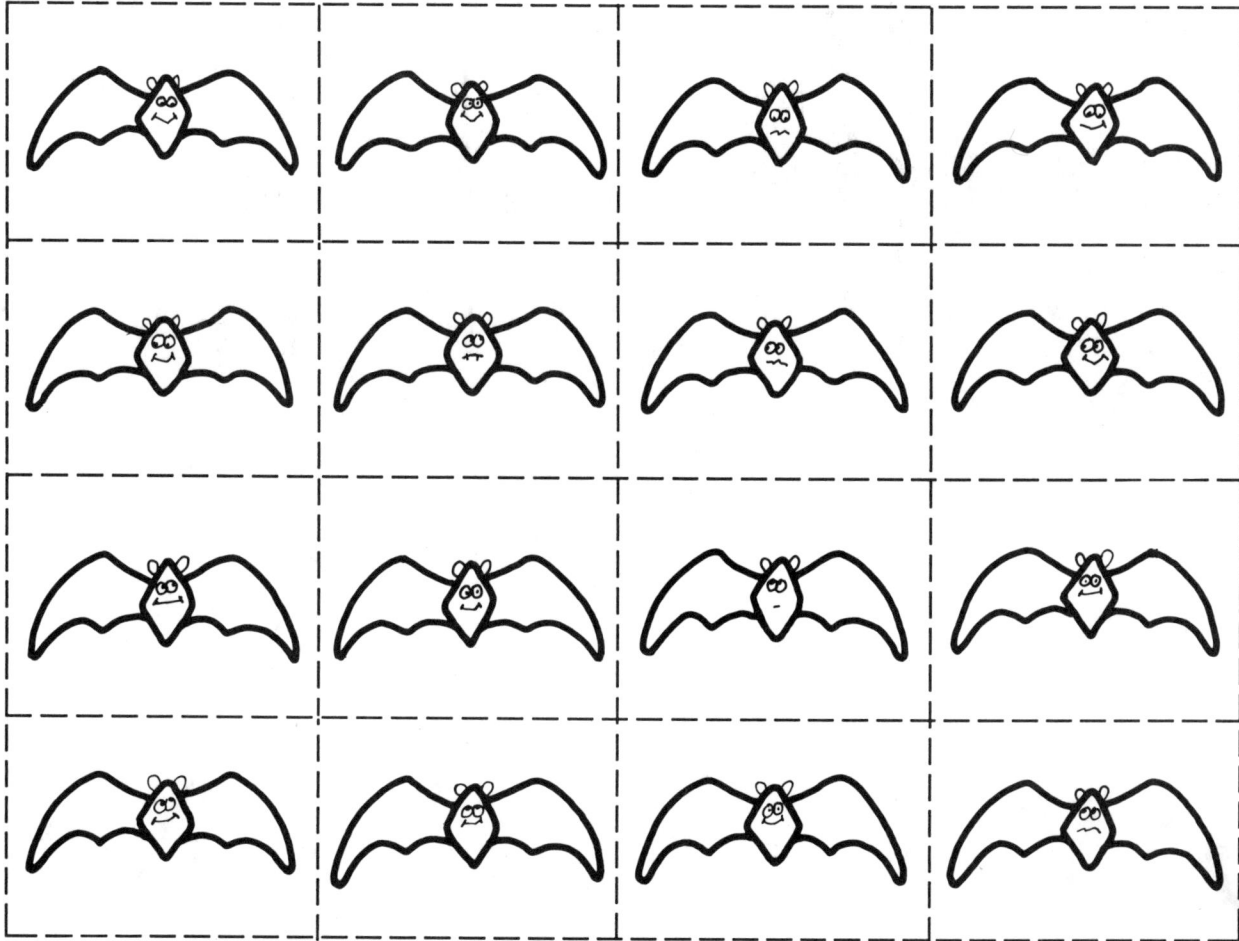

Name: _____

"Batty" Math
✣ ✣ ✣
Solve the problems. Check your work

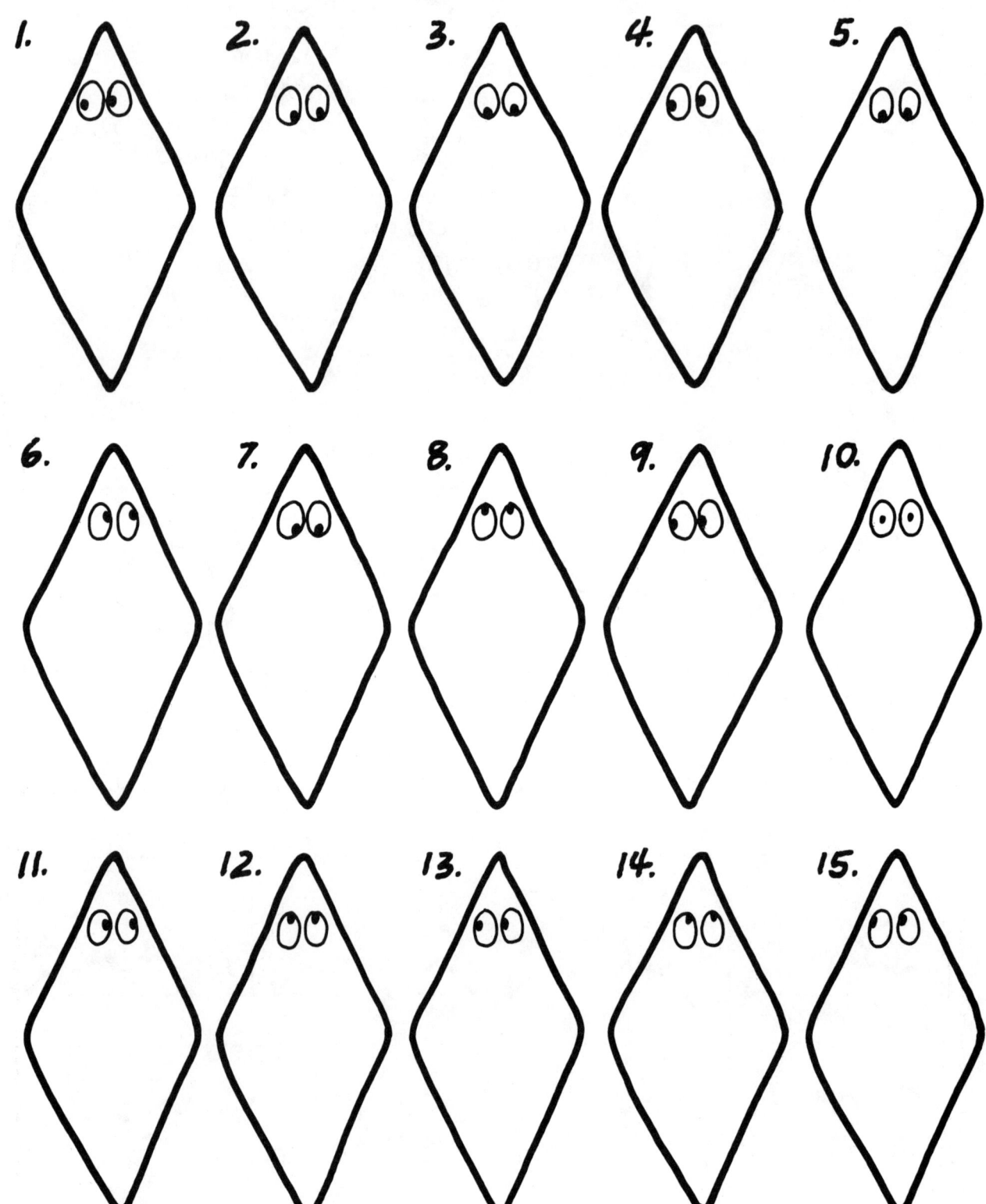

18 "Batty" October

Bat Pattern

Good Work Display

Make one large bat for the corner of the board. Mount students' papers on black construction paper and display. Students can make smaller bats to add to the board.

News for
NOVEMBER TURKEY TIME

Math Lessons

Mr. Turkey
Kindergarten
concept: *shape recognition*
Prepare the following shapes for each child:
- 6" brown circle for turkey body
- 2 1/2" orange square for head
- 8–10 colorful triangles for tail feathers
- 3 small yellow triangles for beak and feet
- 2 small yellow rectangles for legs
- 1 red oval for wattle

Demonstrate how to glue the shapes on a piece of construction paper to make "Mr. Turkey" and have children make their turkeys along with you. Draw a Pilgrim's hat with a black marker and add eyes. Read the following poem or give children a copy to glue next to their "Mr. Turkey."

Here's Thomas Turkey, so big and round.
Look carefully and a circle can be found.
Triangles are so easy to make,
Can you find something that shape?
See his big black Pilgrim hat,
Name a shape that looks like that.
Now, what's the shape of his face?
Surely you'd know that one any place!
Triangles, circle, rectangles, and squares—we're agreed,
Make a fine - looking turkey indeed, indeed!

More Turkey Please!
First and Second Grade
concept: *greater than, less than*
Give each student a copy of "Turkey Talk" (page 24) after you have written a number on each turkey. Have students mark an X on the turkey with the largest number in each pair, or have children write >, <, or = between each pair.

Math Lessons

Turkey Weigh-In
Third Grade
concept: *problem solving*

Give each child a turkey (page 23) and a 7" white circle or paper plate. Let children color and cut out the turkeys. For the feathers, scallop the edges of the 7" circle or plate and color brightly. Glue feathers behind turkey body. Encourage children to be creative and decorate their turkeys with various accessories such as hats, jewelry, and neckties. Have each student glue a small piece of paper on the turkey with its name and weight. Let children choose a partner and show their turkeys to the class. Select a third child to write the two weights on the board and find the sum or difference. Groups of children can come to the front of the room and one child can put the turkeys in order from least to greatest. Or, draw a teeter-totter on the board and have students figure how to put combinations on to balance it.

Think About It . . .
Fourth, Fifth, and Sixth Grade
concept: *word problems*

1. Thomas Turkey weighs 32 pounds. Thorndike Turkey weighs 32 ounces more. How much does he weigh?
2. Tammy Turkey weighs 24 pounds. Timmy Turkey weighs 48 ounces less. What does Timmy weigh?
3. Tina Turkey and Toby Turkey together weigh 36 pounds. Toby's weight is double Tina's. What does Tina weigh? What does Toby weigh?
4. Farmer Brown has 7 turkeys. Each one eats 2 pounds of grain a day. How many pounds will they eat in one week?
5. Farmer Brown's wife will cook Thanksgiving dinner for 20 people. Each person can eat 1/2 pound of turkey. How much should their turkey weigh?
6. The Jones family wants to buy a turkey from Farmer Brown. They will pay him $.98 per pound. They need 50 pounds. How much will their Thanksgiving turkey cost?

Enlarge the turkey pattern (page 26), except for the feathers, and display it on a "Turkey Time" bulletin board. Have the children write word problems on large, bright, construction paper feathers and place them in position around the turkey body. Before Thanksgiving break, have each student take down a feather and read it to the class for discussing and solving.

Border Pattern

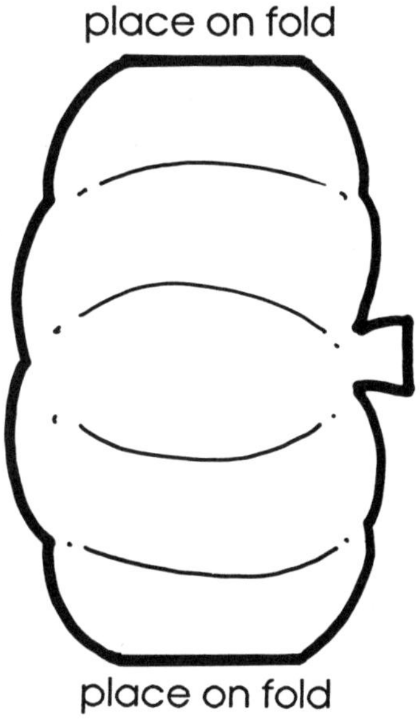

place on fold

place on fold

place on fold

place on fold

Turkey Pattern

November Turkey Time

Name: _____

Turkey Talk

1.

2.

3.

4.

5.

6.

7.

8.

Peek-Over Turkey

Directions: Color the two parts of the picture. Cut on the dotted lines. Glue the four corners of your math paper on a sheet of colored construction paper. Glue the turkey's head on the left corner. Glue its feet at the bottom. Be sure the feet are under its body.

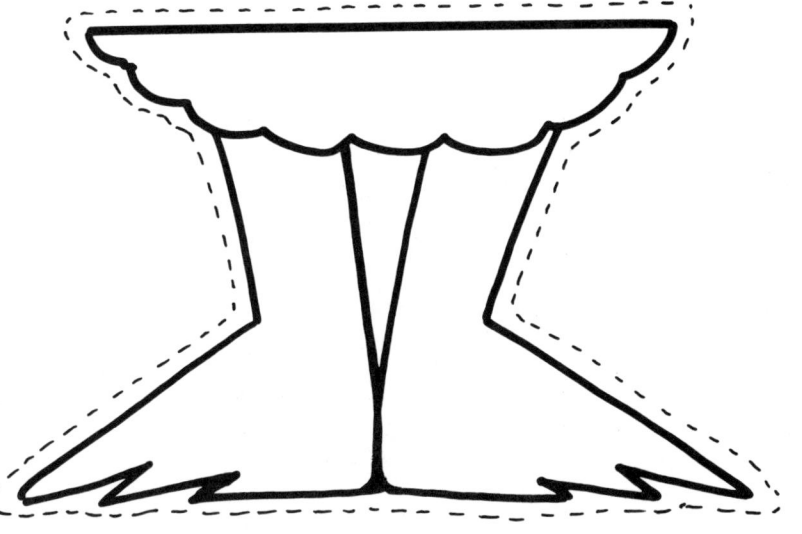

November Turkey Time

Enlarge turkey pattern with overhead projector. Make the body brown, the hat black, the feet and beak yellow, and the wattle red. Cut feathers from colored tissue paper. Staple them in layers behind the turkey body. Leave some loose at the tip to blow in the breeze!

Good Work Display

Delightful "DECEM-BEAR"

Math Lessons

Gifts Galore!
Kindergarten
concept: *counting*
Give each child several gift boxes (page 31) you have prepared with numbers written on the bows. Have children color and cut the boxes out and draw the correct number of gifts inside the boxes or use stickers to represent the numbers.

Bear-y Good Gifts
First and Second Grade
concept: *counting money*
Give each child a gift box, bear, and tag (page 31). Let children color, cut out, and glue items together. Have each student write a price (using large numbers, so they can be easily read) on his or her gift tag.

Display gifts on a bulletin board. Give each gift a number for easier reference. Use the gifts to design thought problems.
1. How much more does gift #4 cost than #5?
2. How much money would you need to buy gifts #2 and #3?
3. If you paid for gift #6 with a $5.00 bill, how much change would you get back?

28 Delightful "Decem-bear"

Math Lessons

Wish Book
Third Grade
concept: *counting money*
Give each child the "Wish Book Money" (page 30) and eight 4" x 6" pieces of construction paper. Let children cut apart the money sentences and glue one on each 4" x 6" piece of paper. Use the eighth piece to make a cover. Staple all pieces together to make a booklet. Have children figure the total amount of each money sentence and write it underneath that sentence. Children can look through old catalogs or magazines and find pictures of things they would like to buy for each amount of money and glue the pictures on the back of the pages.

Think About It . . .
Fourth, Fifth, and Sixth Grade
concept: *word problems*
1. Wrapping paper costs $.85 a roll, or 5 rolls for $4.00. Which is the better buy?
2. Ribbon is $.30 a yard. How much will 48 inches cost?
3. Package ornaments are 2 for $.82. How much will 3 cost?
4. How many feet of 24"-wide paper are needed to wrap a gift that is 20" wide, 2" deep, and 24" tall? (Allow 2" for overlap.)
5. A gift is on sale for 1/2 price. It costs $7.82. What was the original price?
6. A gift weighs 160 ounces. Could you lift it? How many pounds does it weigh?
7. A gift has a circumference of 24". How many feet of ribbon would it take to go around the gift two times?
8. If you began with $5.00 and bought wrapping paper for $1.49, ribbon for $.90, package ornaments for $.58 and a card for $.48, how much would you have left?

Decorate an empty box with wrapping paper and ribbon. Cut a slit in the top. Let students write original thought problems on slips of paper and drop them in the box. During spare classroom minutes, pull one out. Read it aloud and have the class try to answer it. Reward students for especially well-written problems, or reward those who find the answers quickly. Or, create a "Gifts Galore" bulletin board by letting each child write a word problem on a slip of paper and wrap it in a small gift box. Pin all the gifts to the board. On the last day before winter break, let each child take a gift and give it to a friend. Have students open their gifts and solve the word problems inside. After a short time, have the students pass their gifts to another student in a systematic way until all students have worked all the problems.

Delightful "Decem-bear"

Wish • Book • Money

1 dollar, 2 half dollars, 4 quarters, 8 dimes, 6 nickels, and 15 pennies.

120 dimes, 10 nickels, 1 half dollar, and 1 dime.

2 dollars, 1 half dollar, 6 quarters, 21 dimes, 5 nickels, 9 pennies.

21 nickels, 2 one-dollar bills, 3 half dollars, and 1 quarter.

1 five-dollar bill, 21 nickels, and 6 pennies.

10 quarters, 20 nickels, 1 half dollar, and 1 dime.

1 ten-dollar bill, 2 one-dollar bills, 3 quarters, and 6 dimes.

Gift Box

Gift Tag

Gift Bear

Art and Math Throughout the Year © 1989

Delightful "Decem-bear" 31

Name: _____

Practice Presents

✣ ✣ ✣

Solve the problems. Check your work.

32 *Delightful "Decem-bear"*

Peek-Over Bear

Directions: Color the two parts of the picture. Cut on the dotted lines. Glue the four corners of your math paper on a sheet of colored construction paper. Glue the bear's head on the left corner. Glue its feet at the bottom. Be sure the feet are under its body.

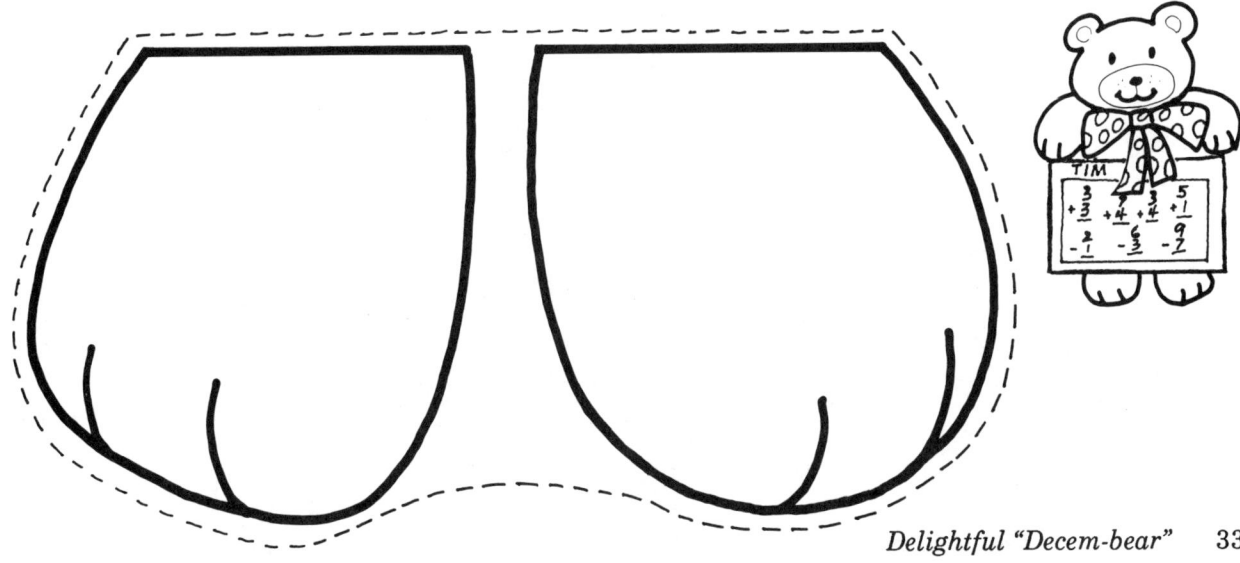

Delightful "Decem-bear"

Border Pattern

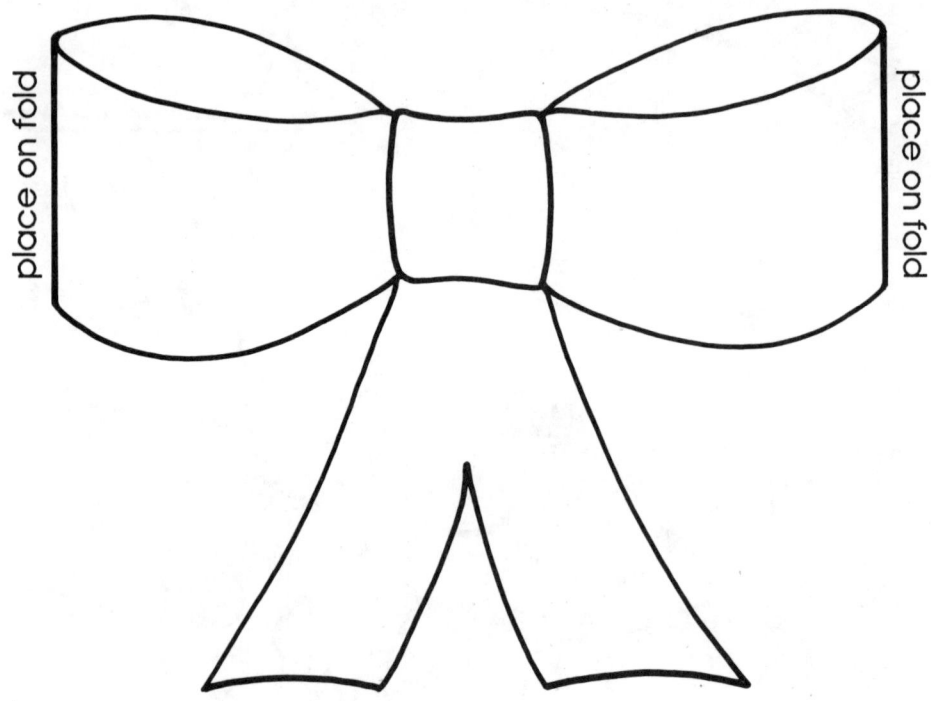

Good Work Display

Enlarge the "peek-over" bear and have him peek over the whole bulletin board. Make the bear's bow out of real ribbon for a 3-D effect.

Delightful "Decem-bear"

January
"Snow" Biz

Math Lessons

Snowman Count
Kindergarten
concept: *number order/sequencing*
Give each child a copy of "Snow" Biz (page 40) and a paper marked off in nine 1" squares with consecutive numbers in each square. Let each child cut the numbers apart and then glue one on each snowman, so the numbers are in sequence from smallest to largest.

Snowball Sculpture
First and Second Grade
concept: *measurement*
Give each child six 4" white snowballs and a copy of "Ways to Measure" (page 39). Let children color, cut out, and glue one measuring tool on each snowball. These snowballs can be used as answer cards. Ask the following questions, and have children hold up snowballs to indicate their answers.
- How would you measure how cold it is outside on a snowy day?
- How would you measure how tall your snowman is?
- How would you measure melted snow?
- How would you know when to stop playing and go inside?
- How would you know when it will be Saturday?
- How would you measure the weight of your biggest snowball?

Then let each child make a snowball sculpture by gluing the measurement snowballs on a 9" x 12" piece of construction paper. Display sculptures on a bulletin board. Children can cut out snowflakes to add to the board.

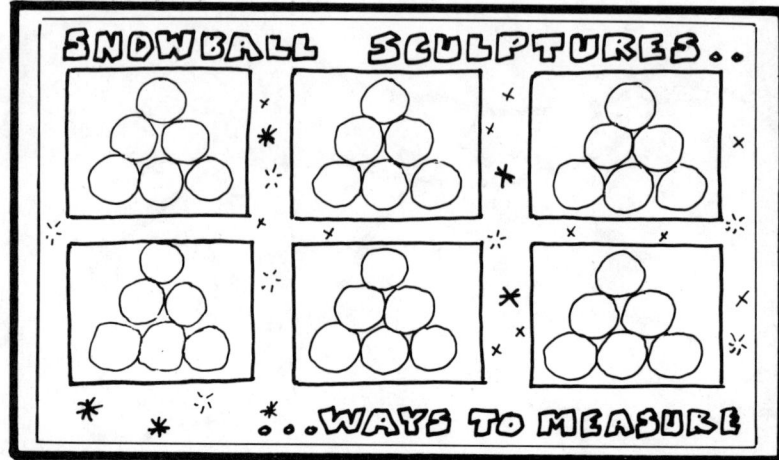

Math Lessons

Blizzard Bunch
Third Grade
concept: *multiplication*

Give each child a "Blizzard Bunch" snowman (page 38) to color, cut out, and glue together. Have each child write a basic multiplication problem on the snowman's body and the product on the small snowball.

Display the snowmen on a bulletin board with half on one side and half on the other to give the appearance of a snowball fight. Pin all the snowballs in the center of the board. Students can take turns pinning the snowballs in the correct snowman's hand. Or, some morning, have all the snowballs pinned up correctly except for two. See who is the first to notice the mistake!

Think About It...
Fourth, Fifth, and Sixth Grade
concept: *word problems*

1. If a snow ice cream recipe called for 4 cups of snow, how many pints of snow would you need?
2. If you were making half of a recipe and it called for 1/2 cup of milk, how much milk would you need?
3. If one person could eat half of the ice cream the recipe made, how many people could be served if the recipe were doubled?
4. If a recipe called for 1/4 teaspoon of vanilla and you wanted to double the recipe, how much vanilla would you need?
5. If you had a pint of milk and you used 1/2 cup in a recipe, how much would you have left?
6. If you made 3 gallons of ice cream, how many quart-size containers would you need to store it in?
7. If you had a quart of ice cream and you served 3 guests one cup each, how much ice cream would you have left?

January "Snow" Biz 37

Blizzard Bunch Snowman

snowball

hat

body

scarf

head

38 January "Snow" Biz

Ways • to • Measure

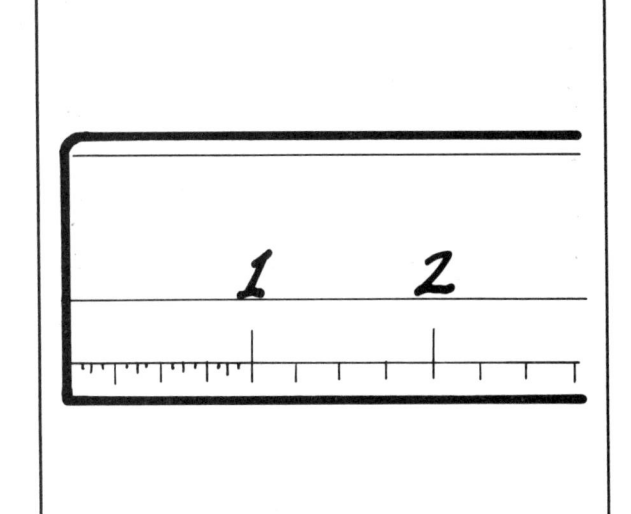

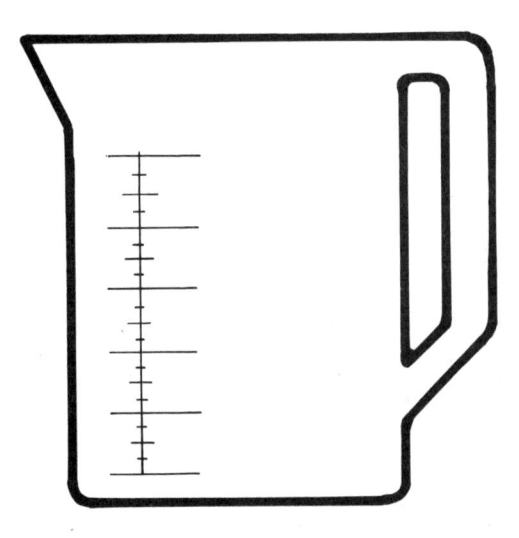

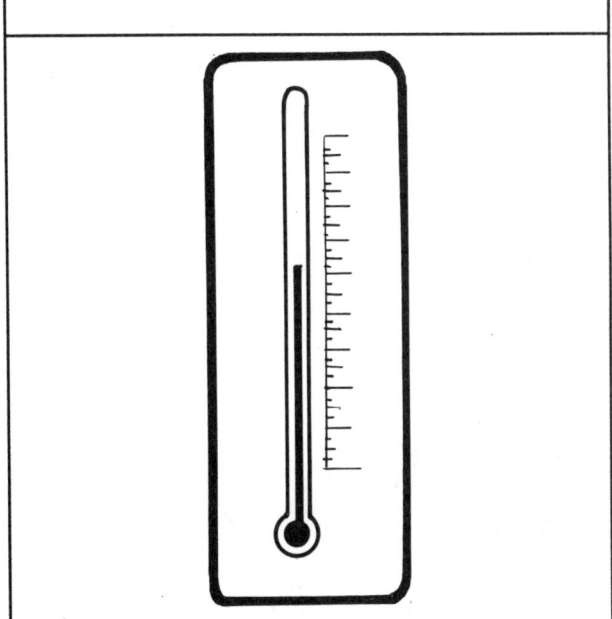

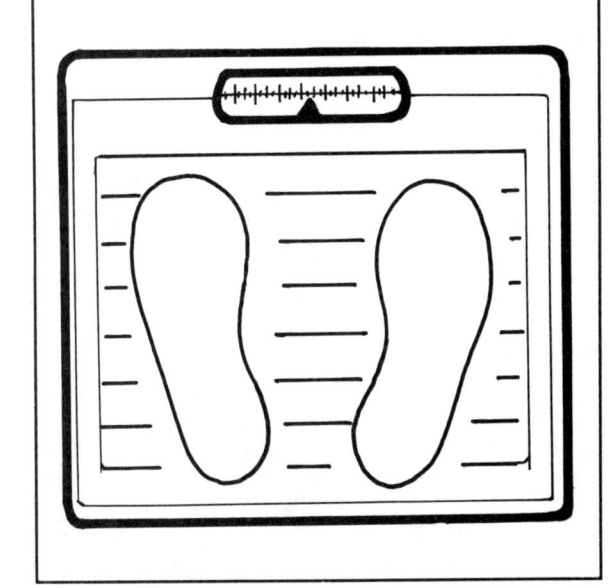

Name: _____

"Snow" Biz

40 January "Snow" Biz

Peek-Over Snowman

Directions: Color and cut out the snowman. Cut the arm along the dotted line. Glue the four corners of your math paper on a piece of colored construction paper. Slip your paper under the snowman's arm and glue in place.

January "Snow" Biz

Good Work Display

Enlarge snowman and display on a blue bulletin board background. Use fabric to make scarf and mittens. Mount "cool" work papers on sheets of white construction paper with icicle-shaped bottoms. Students can make snowflakes to scatter around.

42   January "Snow" Biz

Heart-y
FEBRUARY FUN!

Math Lessons

Hearts, Hearts, Hearts
Kindergarten
concept: *addition facts*
Give each child a copy of "Hearts, Hearts, Hearts" (page 46) after you have written in six addition problems. Let children color the hearts to represent the addends and then write the sums in the blanks.

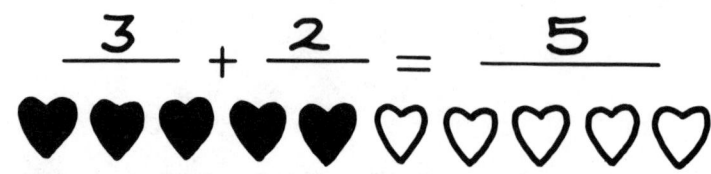

$$\underline{3} + \underline{2} = \underline{5}$$
♥♥♥♥♥♡♡♡♡♡

Happy Hearts
First and Second Grade
concept: *union of sets*
Give each child a heart, shoe, and hand pattern (page 49) to trace and cut out of red, pink, or white paper. Give each child four 3/4" x 3" paper strips. Have each child fold strips accordion-style and use for the arms and legs to attach the feet and hands to the heart. Children can draw happy faces on their hearts.

Use yarn to construct a large, overlapping square, circle, and triangle on a bulletin board. Display "happy hearts" on the board. Ask questions such as:
- How many hearts are in the circle?
- How many hearts are shared by the triangle and the circle?
- How many hearts are shared by the square and the triangle?
- How many hearts are not in the square?

44 *Heart-y February Fun!*

Math Lessons

Heart-y Party
Third Grade
concept: *money*

As a class, think of treats and supplies that would be necessary for a "heart-y" Valentine party. List them on the board. Then add a price to each item. Your list may include:
- cookies $1.50 per dozen
- lollipops $.10 each
- decorations $5.98 per pkg.
- pop $2.25
- heart candy $1.98 per bag

Give each child a box pattern (page 47). Let each child choose 6 party items and draw one on each side of the box and write the price for each. Cut the box out and fold on all lines. Glue Tab A to Side A, then Tab B to Side B, and finally Tab C to Side C. Choose 3 students to bring their finished boxes to the front of the room and roll them like dice on a table. Have them each call out the price that lands on the top. Have other children quickly figure the total for the three items. The first person to figure correctly can be next to roll his or her box along with two chosen friends.

Think About It . . .
Fourth, Fifth, and Sixth Grade
concept: *word problems*

FACT: A small heart usually beats faster than a larger heart. This is true for animals too. An elephant's heart may beat only 25 times per minute, while a mouse's heart may beat 700 times per minute.
- ♥ FIGURE how many more times per hour a mouse's heart will beat than an elephant's heart.

FACT: The human body has about one quart of blood for every 25 pounds.
- ♥ FIGURE how many quarts of blood your body has.
- ♥ FIGURE how many pints of blood your body has.

FACT: Human hearts weigh about 2/3 of 1% of a person's weight.
- ♥ FIGURE the weight of your heart.

FACT: The resting pulse rate of an average adult is 72 times per minute.
- ♥ FIGURE how many times an average adult's heart will beat in one hour and in one day.

FACT: The resting pulse rate of a well-conditioned adult is only 42 times per minute.
- ♥ FIGURE how many beats a well-conditioned heart can save in one minute, or in one hour, or in one day.

Make a "Heart-y Facts and Figures" bulletin board. Let children work in groups to make large hearts. Provide glitter, yarn, lace, etc. Have them write a fact on one heart and a problem to figure on another. Display hearts on the bulletin board.

Name: _____

Hearts, Hearts, Hearts
♥ ♥ ♥
Color the hearts. Write the sum.

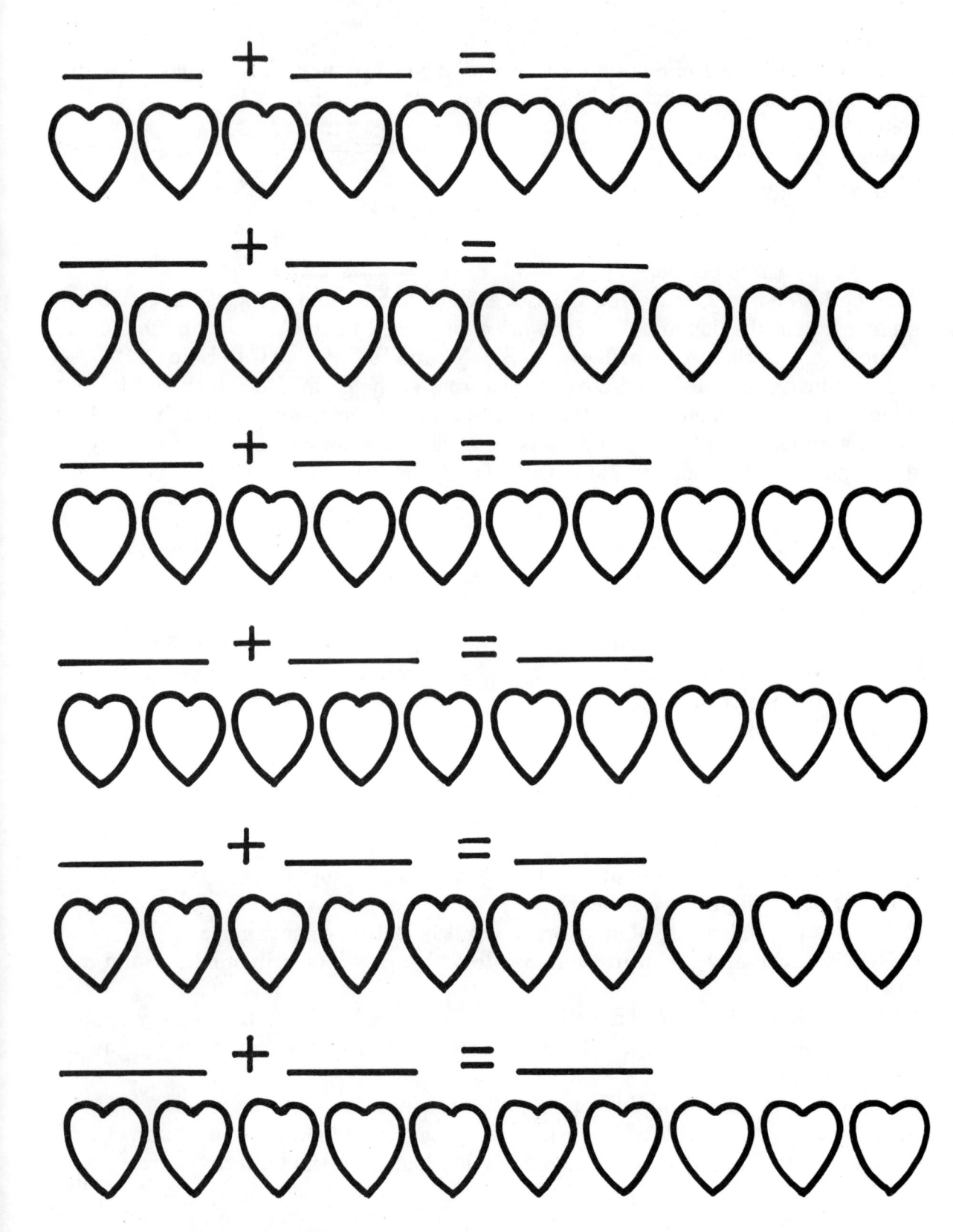

___ + ___ = ___

♡♡♡♡♡♡♡♡♡♡

___ + ___ = ___

♡♡♡♡♡♡♡♡♡♡

___ + ___ = ___

♡♡♡♡♡♡♡♡♡♡

___ + ___ = ___

♡♡♡♡♡♡♡♡♡♡

___ + ___ = ___

♡♡♡♡♡♡♡♡♡♡

___ + ___ = ___

♡♡♡♡♡♡♡♡♡♡

Heart-y February Fun!

Heart-y Party Box

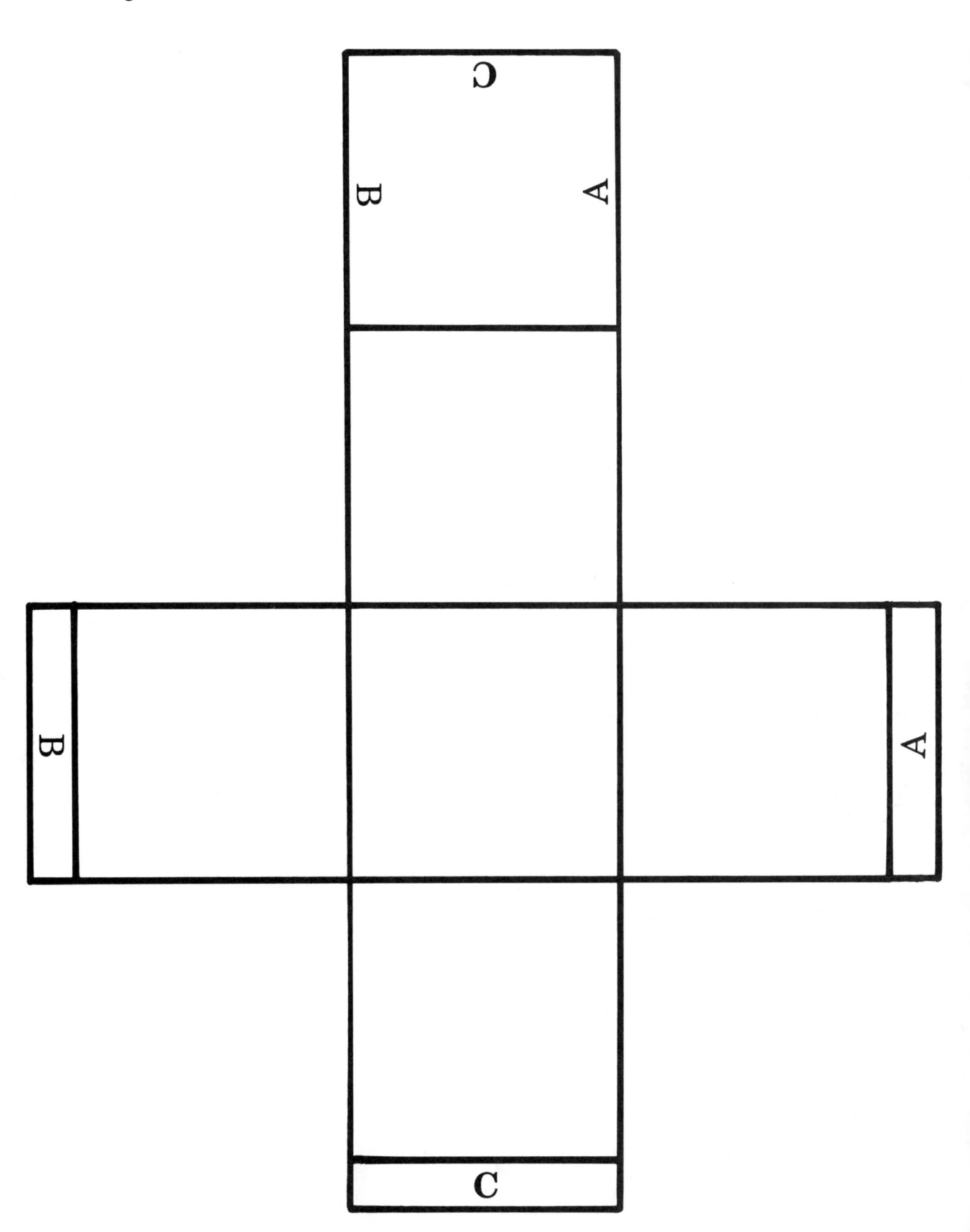

Heart-y February Fun!

Name: _____

"Have a Heart"
❤ ❤ ❤
Solve the problems. Check your work.

1. 2. 3. 4.

5. 6. 7. 8.

9. 10. 11. 12.

13. 14. 15. 16.

Heart-y February Fun!

Border Pattern

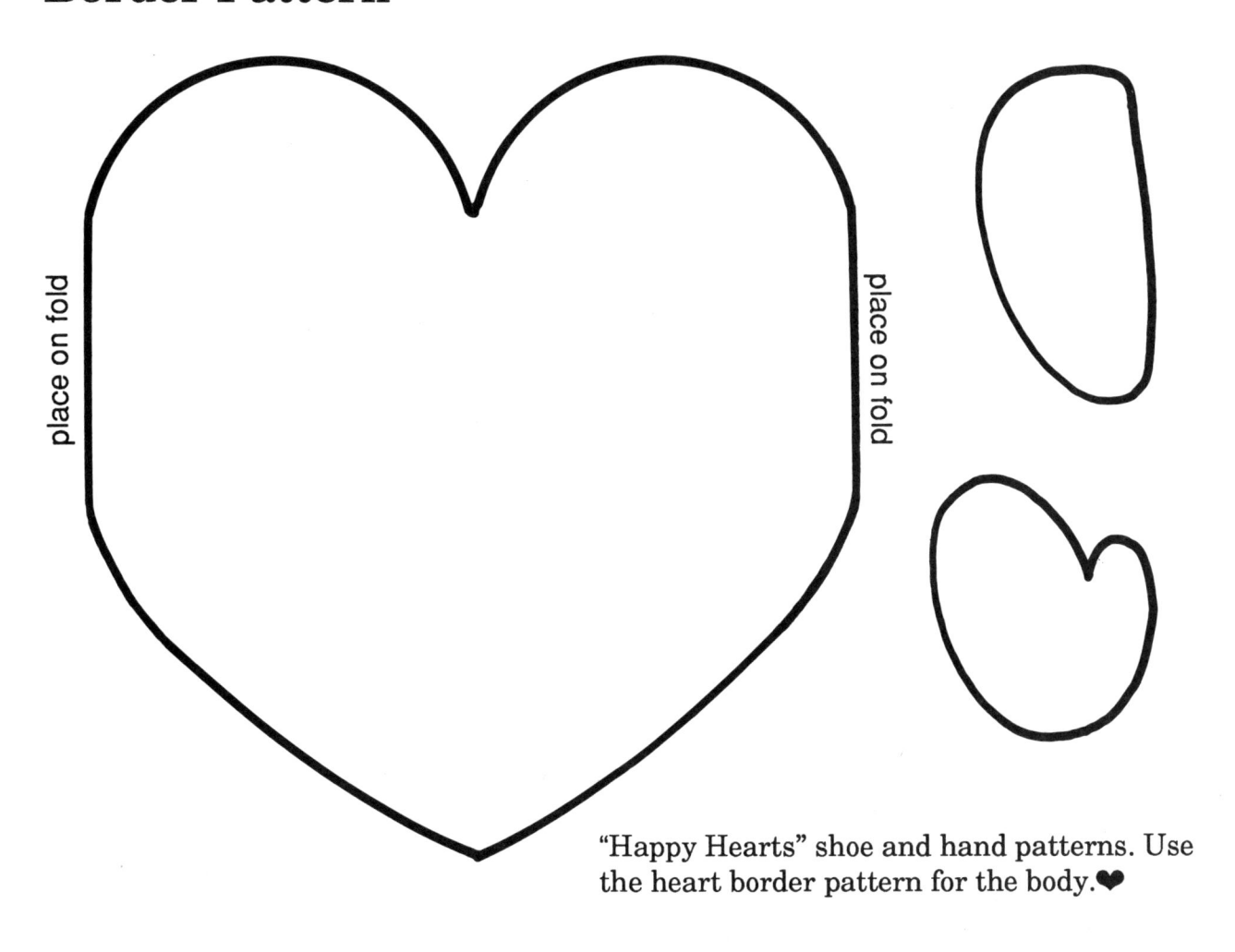

place on fold

place on fold

"Happy Hearts" shoe and hand patterns. Use the heart border pattern for the body.

Good Work Display

Enlarge patterns above to make one large "happy heart." Use a long narrow rectangle and a large square to make a black hat. Display student papers with a heart attached to the upper left corner of each paper. Let students put their names on the hearts, using glitter for a sparkling touch!

Heart-y February Fun!

March/April
Funny Bunnies!

Math Lessons

Funny Bunny Families
Kindergarten
concept: *addition facts*

Give each child a "Funny Bunny" (page 53) to color, cut out, and glue together. Let each child glue on a small piece of cotton for a fluffy tail. Display several larger bunnies with a sum on each apron on a bulletin board. Have children write equations on the bunny heads to match a sum on a larger bunny's apron and display them also.

Enlarge with overhead projector.

Egg Hunt
First and Second Grade
concept: *number patterns*

Give each child an egg pattern (page 57). Let each child trace and cut out four eggs on colored construction paper. Have children think of number sequences counting by ones, twos, fives, or tens and write one number on each egg. Each child should leave one egg blank and decorate it with beautiful, bright colors. Have each child glue the four eggs on a construction paper strip in sequence, using the colored egg as a placeholder for the missing number. Use the strips as classroom flashcards. Hold up a strip and let children name the number that should go on the colored egg. Or, display the patterns on an "Egg Hunt" bulletin board to provide daily reinforcement.

March/April Funny Bunnies

Math Lessons

Funny Bunny Fractions
Third Grade
concept: *fractions*

Give each child a string of bunnies (page 54). Children can trim the strings to make them shorter or add bunnies to make them longer. Have children color some bunnies and leave others white. Cotton can be used for the tails. Then, have each child write a fraction on a 3" x 5" card to represent the amount of shaded bunnies on his or her string. Display bunny strings on a bulletin board and match the appropriate 3" x 5" cards underneath.

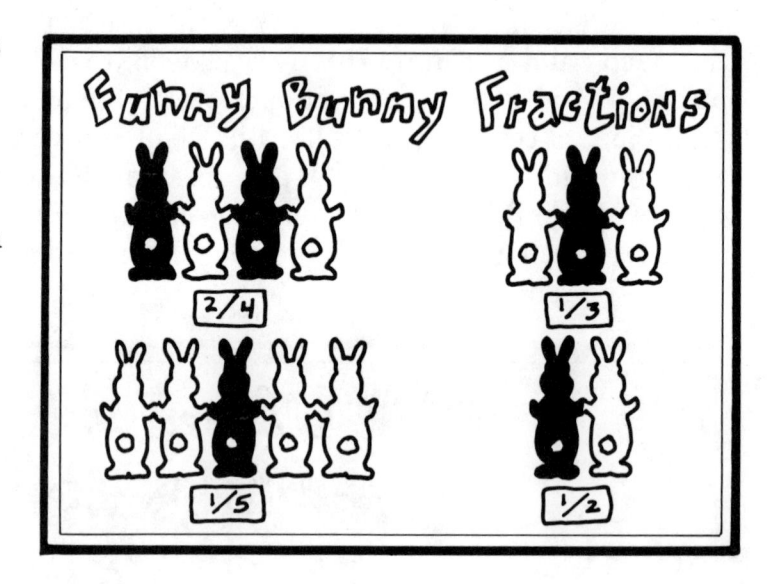

Think About It . . .
Fourth, Fifth, and Sixth Grade
concept: *word problems*

1. Harry has 33 white hares. He has three white hares for every two brown hares. How many brown hares does he have?
2. One hare hopped around the house in 62.4 seconds. He improved his time by 0.01 second each day for three days. What was his hopping speed after the three days?
3. Harry fed his baby hares 18.5 grams of food the first week, 25 grams the second week, 31.5 grams the third week. He increased the food by the same amount each week. How much will he feed them the fourth week?
4. One hare can hop one kilometer in two days. How many meters can he hop in four days.
5. Harry's "hoppingest" hare can hop 200 centimeters in one hop. How many hops will it take him to hop a distance of six meters?
6. Harry's heaviest hare weighs 20,000 grams. How many kilograms does he weigh?

Let each student print a different "hare-y" word problem on an egg-shaped piece of paper. Some problems are suggested above and students can make up their own. Put one egg on each student's desk and number the eggs in consecutive order. Have each student "hop" one desk to the right each time you give a signal and answer the word problem on a numbered answer sheet. Be sure students write their answers in the numbered spots on the answer sheets that correspond with the numbers on the eggs. When students are back at their own desks, they will have answered all the problems and filled their entire answer sheet.

Funny • Bunny • Patterns

Use cotton for a fluffy tail!

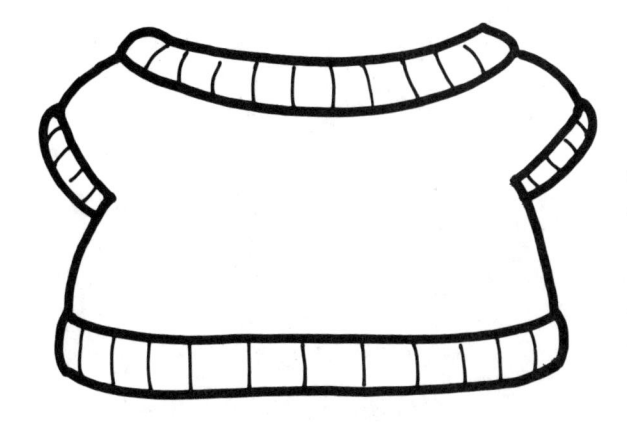

5+0   4+1

Art and Math Throughout the Year © 1989

March/April Funny Bunnies   53

Funny Bunny Fraction Strings

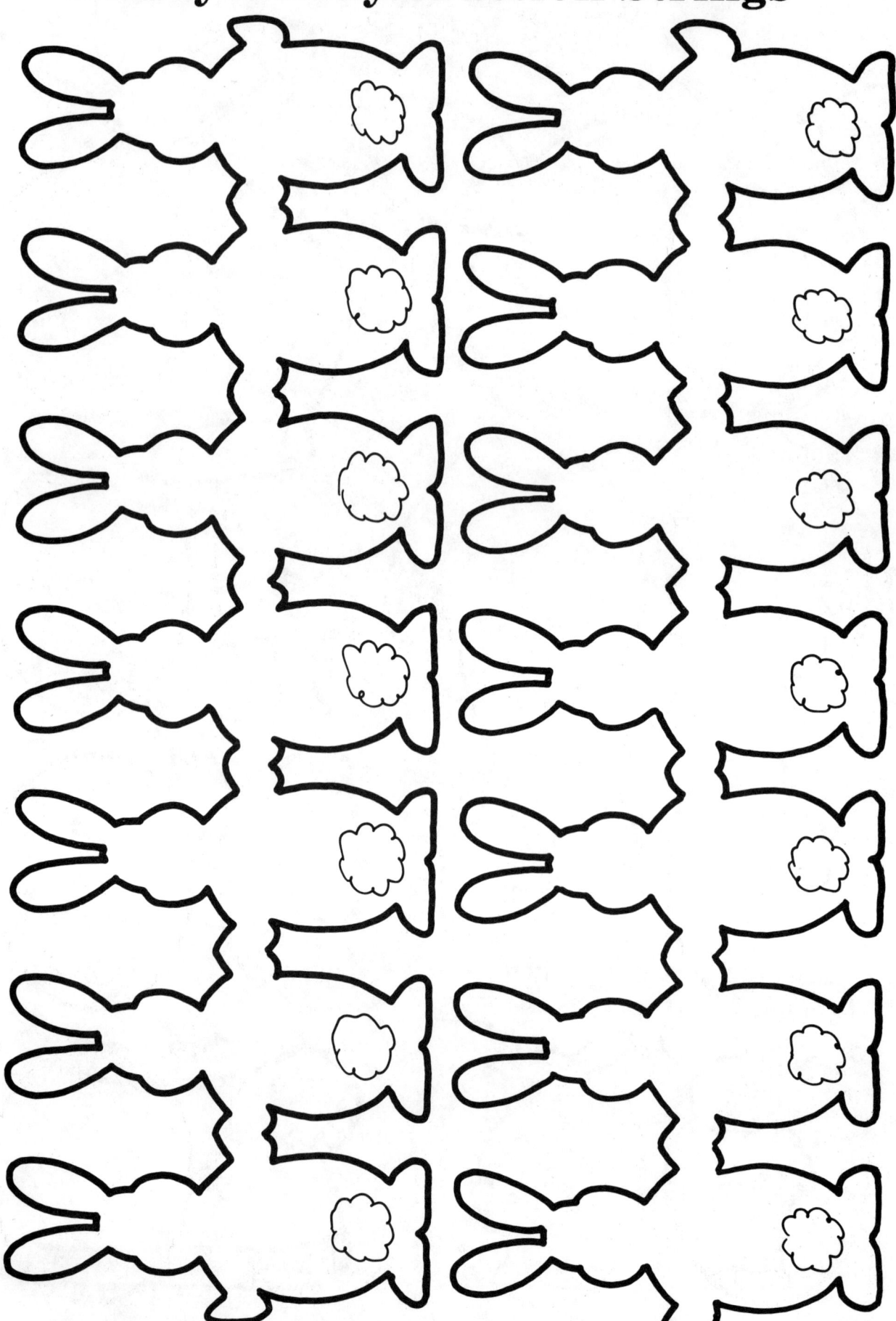

54 *March/April Funny Bunnies*

Name: _____

"Egg" stra Practice
✣ ✣ ✣
Solve the problems. Check your work.

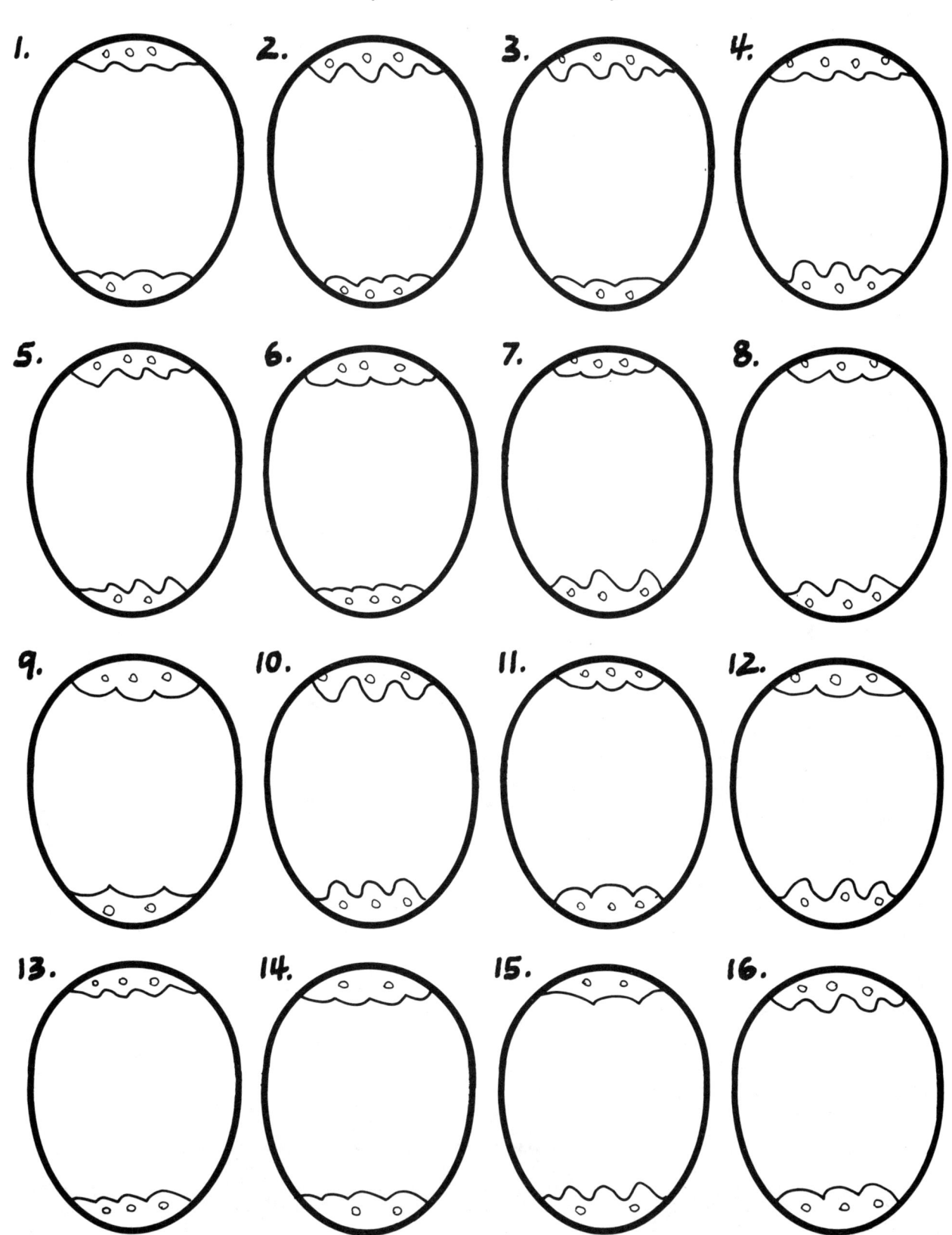

1. 2. 3. 4.

5. 6. 7. 8.

9. 10. 11. 12.

13. 14. 15. 16.

March/April Funny Bunnies 55

Peek-Over Bunny

Directions: Color the two parts of the picture. Cut on the dotted lines. Glue the four corners of your math paper on a sheet of colored construction paper. Glue the bunny's head on the left corner. Glue its feet at the bottom. Be sure the feet are under its body.

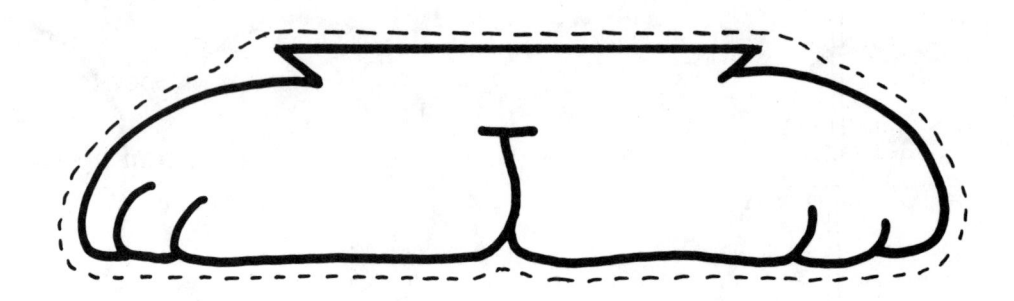

56 *March/April Funny Bunnies*

Border Pattern

Let children decorate each string of eggs before using them as a border.

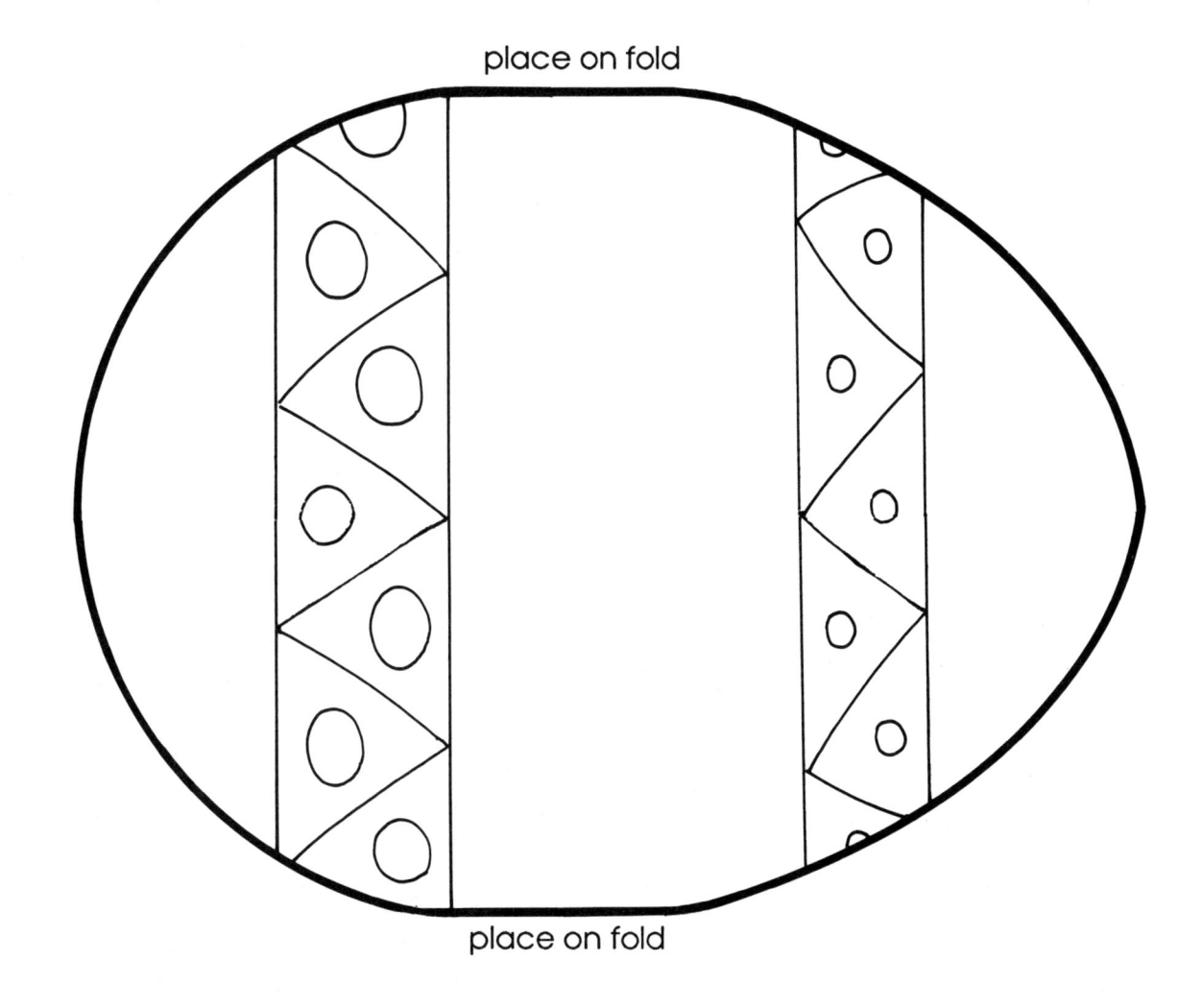

place on fold

place on fold

Good Work Display

Enlarge the "peek-over" bunny with an overhead projector and have him peek over the whole bulletin board. Use pink felt for his nose and inner ears.

March/April Funny Bunnies

May
Blooming Brightly!

Math Lessons

Petal Power
Kindergarten
concept: *addition facts*
Give each child a flower (page 64) with a simple addition problem written in its center to color and cut out. Let each child glue the flower on a piece of construction paper and draw a stem. Provide a pile of pre-cut, green construction paper leaves. Each child should choose the appropriate number of leaves to glue on his or her stem, to represent the sum of the addition problem. Display the artwork on a "Petal Power" bulletin board.

Flower Fun
First and Second Grade
concept: *pictographs*
Give each child twenty-four 5" squares of red, yellow, blue, or purple tissue paper. Direct each child to accordion-pleat together a stack of eight squares and tightly wrap a piece of pipe cleaner around the middle, twisting the pipe cleaner ends together. Trim the edges to round the corners. Carefully pull each tissue sheet up towards the center on both sides of the pipe cleaner to fluff out the flower. Each child should make three flowers of the same color.

Display one flower from each child on a pictograph bulletin board in rows by color. Ask students questions such as:
- How many flowers did you make?
- How many of the flowers you made are on the board? (Have them discover that each flower on the pictograph represents three actual flowers.)
- How many flowers are red?
- How many more flowers are blue than purple?
- How many more yellow flowers are needed to equal the number of blue flowers?
- How many blue and yellow flowers are there altogether?

May Blooming Brightly

Math Lessons

Spring Things
Third Grade
concept: *ordered pairs*

As a class, make a list of spring "things." Your list might include: butterfly, rose, bee, daffodil, ladybug, daisy, rain, hummingbird, sun, or tulip. List one spring "thing" for each child in the class. Let each child choose one "thing," draw and color it on a 4" x 4" piece of paper, and cut it out.

Using yarn, prepare a grid on a bulletin board. Number the grid across the bottom and up the left side. Call out a child's name and an ordered pair of numbers (2,7) and have the child place his spring "thing" on the board in that spot. When each child has had his or her turn, ask other questions to practice locating coordinate points: Where is the sun? Where is the ladybug?

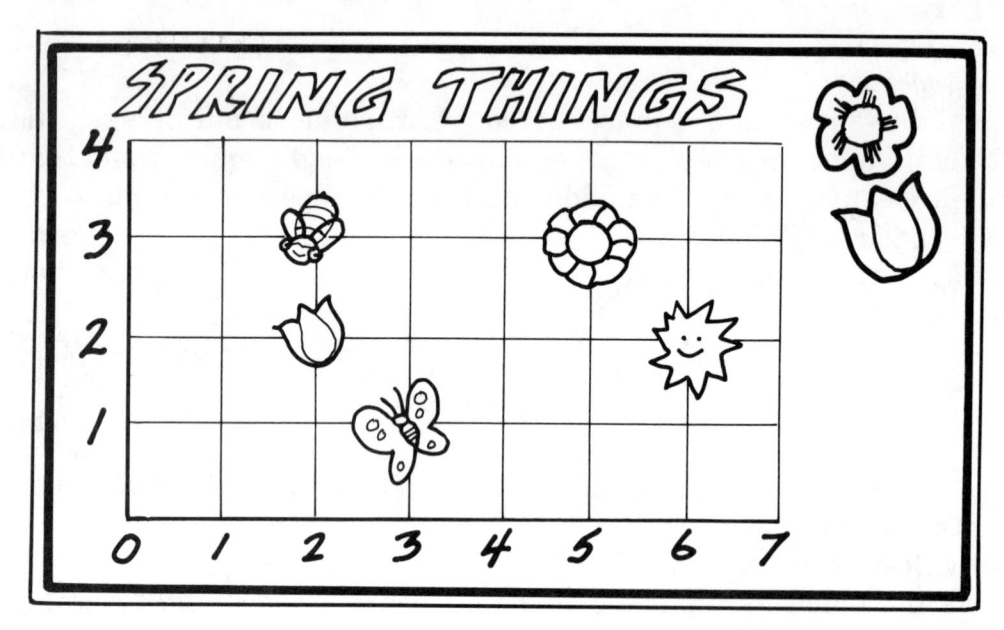

Think About It . . .
Fourth, Fifth, and Sixth Grade
concept: *word problems*

1. Maybelle May worked in her garden two hours on Monday, three hours on Tuesday hours, five hours on Wednesday, two hours on Thursday, and seven hours on Friday. How many hours did she work? What is the average number of hours she worked per day?
2. Mrs. May's garden is planted as follows: sunflowers 3/8, tulips 1/16, daffodils 1/4, and the rest daisies. What fractional part of the garden is planted with daisies?
3. What is the area of a rectangular 10' x 25' garden?
4. If Mrs. May sold three daffodils for $1.75 each, how much would a dozen cost?
5. If Mrs. May sells tulips for $.45 each, will she make more money selling a dozen tulips or a dozen daffodils?
6. How many feet of fence must Mrs. May buy to fence her 10' x 25' garden?

60   *May Blooming Brightly*

Patterns

May Blooming Brightly

Peek-Over Bee

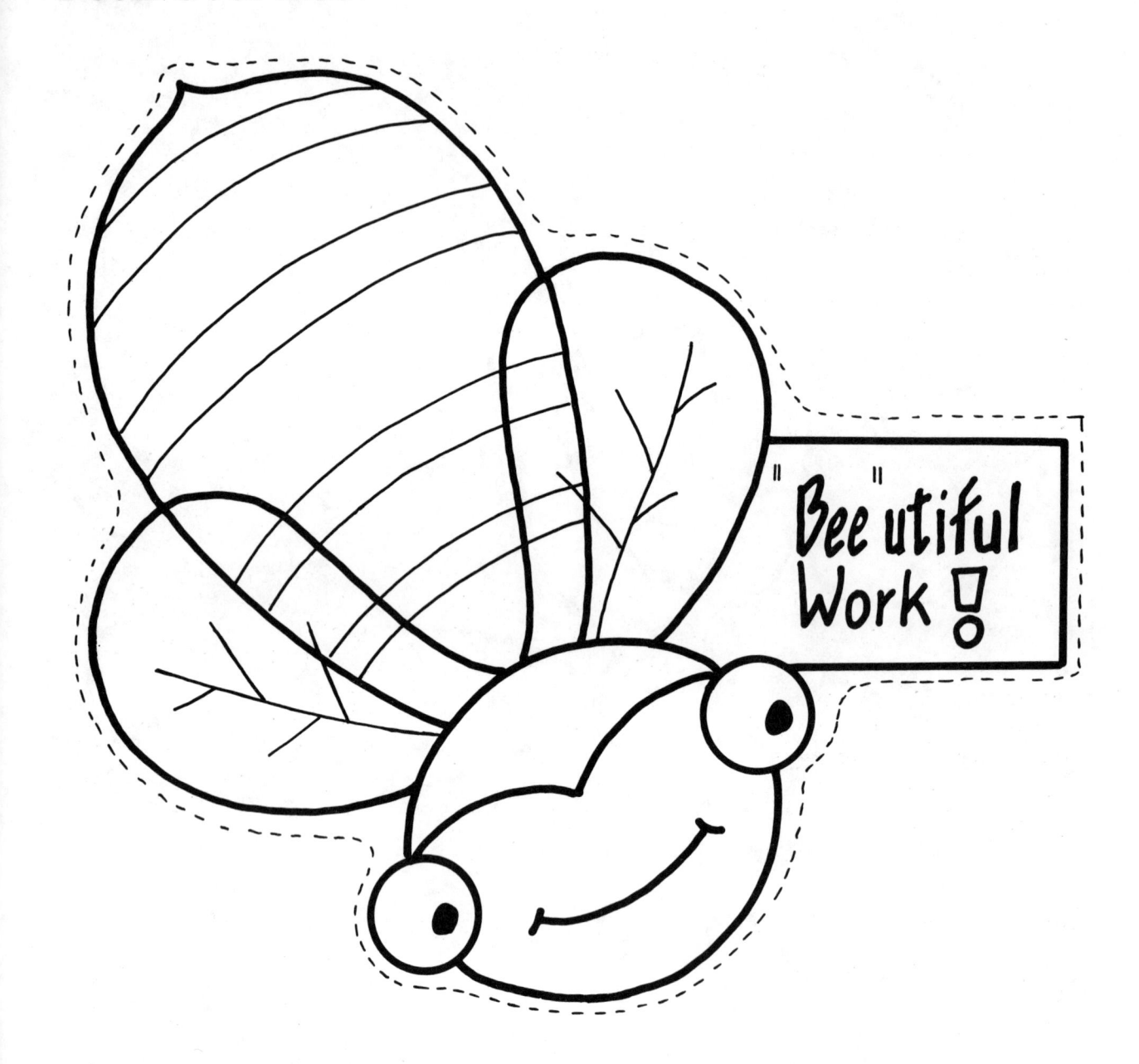

"Bee"utiful Work !

Directions: Color the bee and cut on the dotted lines. Glue the four corners of your math paper on a sheet of colored construction paper. Glue the bee on the left corner of your paper.

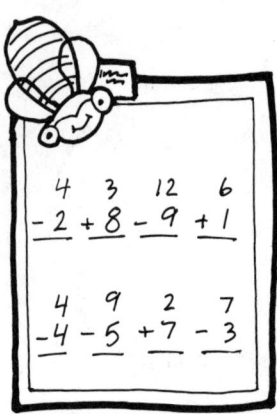

62   May Blooming Brightly

Name:_____

Flower Power
✤ ✤ ✤
Solve the problems. Check your work.

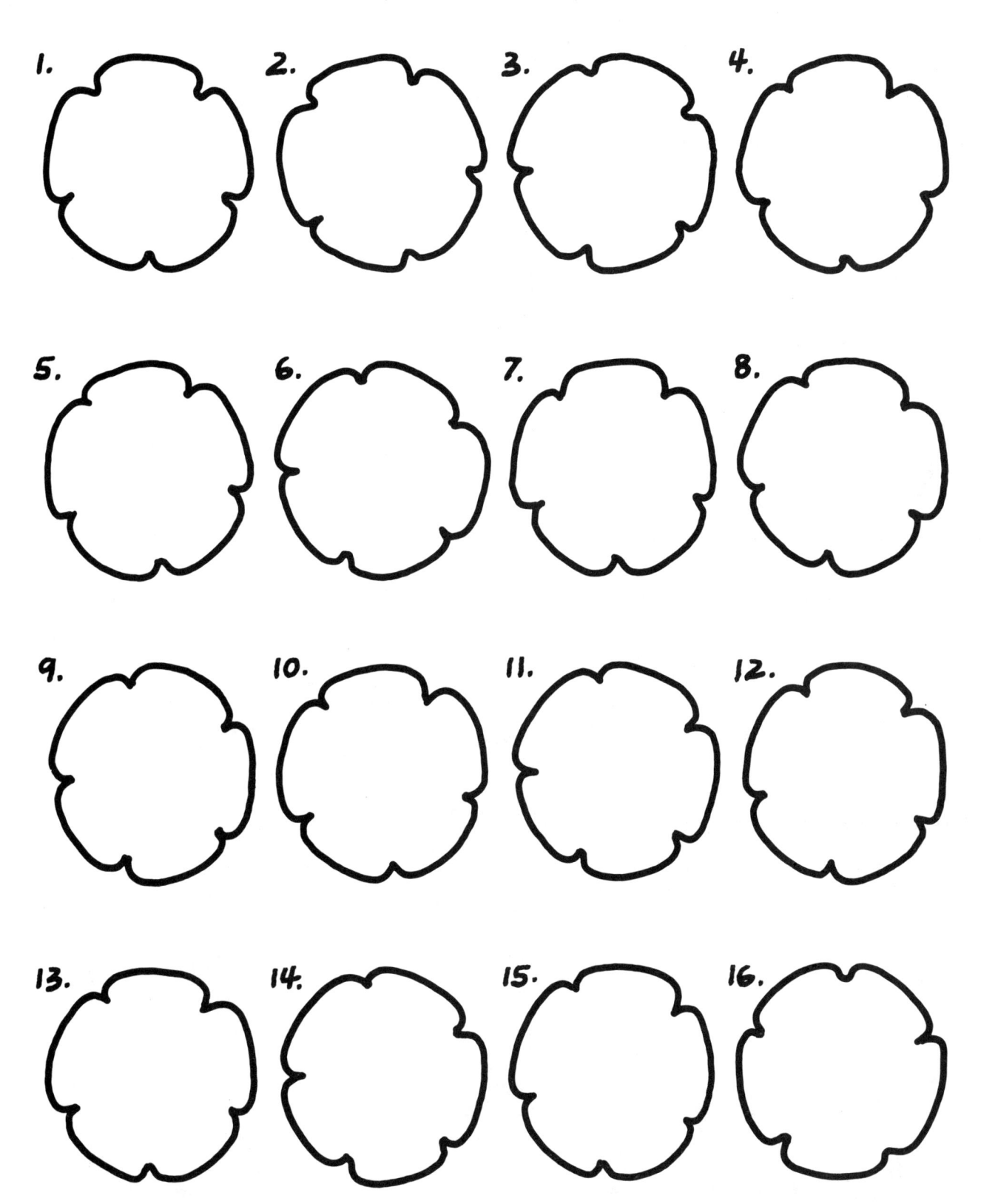

1.
2.
3.
4.
5.
6.
7.
8.
9.
10.
11.
12.
13.
14.
15.
16.

May Blooming Brightly

Border Pattern

Let children add little yellow centers to each string of flowers for an added touch of spring!

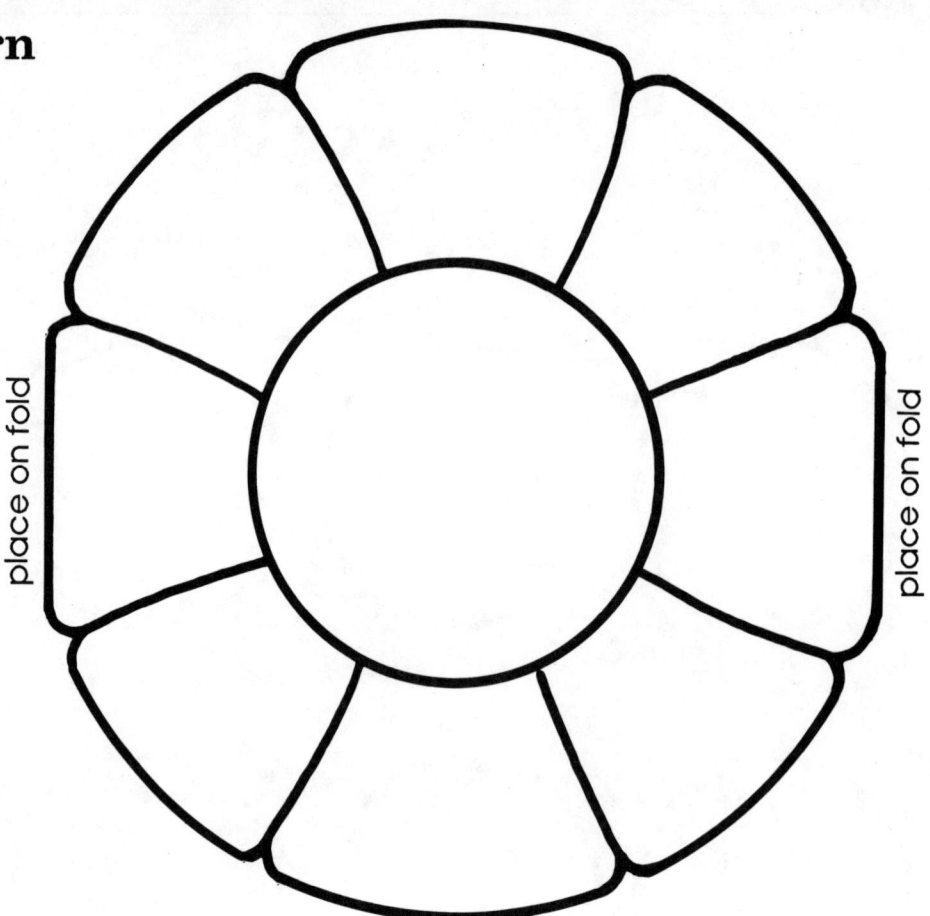

place on fold

place on fold

Good Work Display

Enlarge patterns on page 61 for bulletin board display. Let children color and cut them out.

Something to Buzz About

64   *May Blooming Brightly*

Art and Math Throughout the Year © 1989